book
3

Composition Practice

THIRD EDITION

A Text for English Language Learners

Linda Lonon Blanton
University of New Orleans
New Orleans, Louisiana

THOMSON

™

HEINLE

United States • Australia • Canada • Mexico • Singapore • Spain • United Kingdom

THOMSON
HEINLE

Composition Practice, Book 3, Third Edition
Linda Lonon Blanton

Vice President, Editorial Director ESL/EFL: Nancy Leonhardt
Acquisitions Editor: Sherrise Roehr
Managing Editor: James W. Brown
Revision Writer: Janet Podnecki
Sr. Production Editor: Maryellen Killeen
Sr. Marketing Manager: Charlotte Sturdy
Sr. Manufacturing Coordinator: Mary Beth Hennebury

Composition: A Plus Publishing Services
Project Management: Anita Raducanu
Photo Research: Lisa LaFortune
Illustration: Scott MacNeill
Cover Design: Gina Petti, Rotunda Design
Text Design: Julia Gecha
Printer: Mazer Corporation

For permission to use material from this text or product contact us:
Tel   1-800-730-2214
Fax   1-800-730-2215
Web   www.thomsonrights.com

Library of Congress Cataloging-in-Publication Data
Blanton, Linda Lonon
    Composition practice : a text for English language learners / Linda Lonon Blanton.--3rd ed.
       p. cm.
    ISBN: 0-8384-1999-2 (bk. 3 : pbk.)
       1. English language--Textbooks for foreign speakers.
    2. English language--Composition and exercises.
    I. Title.

PE1128.B5894 2001
808′.042--dc21

                                        2001016700

International Division List

ASIA (excluding India)
Thomson Learning
5 Shenton Way #01-01
UIC Building
Singapore 068808

AUSTRALIA/NEW ZEALAND
Nelson/Thomson Learning
102 Dodds Street
South Melbourne
Victoria 3205 Australia

CANADA
Nelson/Thomson Learning
1120 Birchmount Road
Scarborough, Ontario
Canada M1K 5G4

LATIN AMERICA
Thomson Learning
Seneca, 53
Colonia Polanco
11560 México D.F. México

SPAIN
Thomson Learning
Calle Magallanes, 25
28015-Madrid
España

UK/EUROPE/MIDDLE EAST
Thomson Learning
Berkshire House
168-173 High Holborn
London, WC1V 7AA, United Kingdom

Photo Credits:
2, © Dallas & John Heaton/Stock Boston; 3, (TL) © Tibor Bognar/The Stock Market, (BL) © George Shelley/The Stock Market, (BR) © Bachmann/Stock Boston; 14, © Richard Pasley/Stock Boston; 16, © Jim Corwin/Stock Boston; 15, © Ruth Dixon, Stock Boston; 20, © Bettmann/CORBIS; 30, © Bob Rowan; Progressive Image/CORBIS; 46, © Spencer Grant, Stock Boston; 49, Heinle & Heinle Image Resource Bank; 50, © Spencer Grant, Stock Boston; 62, © Bob Daemmrich, Stock Boston; 76, Grant LeDuc/Stock Boston; 77 (T) Martin Rogers, (B) © Wolfgang Kaehler/CORBIS; 79, © David Ulmer/Stock Boston; 89, Ulrike Welsch, Stock Boston; 92, (T) Mark Humphrey/World Wide, (B) © Dave G. Houser/CORBIS; 106 & 107, © Paul Barton, The Stock Market; 109, © Ellis Herwig/Stock Boston; 120, © Bob Daemmrich, Stock Boston; 121, (L) © Davis Factor/CORBIS, (R) © Laura Dwight/CORBIS; 126, © Charles Gupton, Stock Boston; 134, Magnum; 135, © Jerry Cooke/CORBIS.

Preface

This third edition of *Composition Practice, Book 3*, celebrates the continuing successful use of the series by many thousands of English learners. Prepared for intermediate-level students of English who plan to use the language for academic and professional purposes, *Composition Practice, Book 3*, retains its original instructional design and pedagogy. In response to user suggestions, the language level of the readings that open each unit has been simplified somewhat to allow for a smoother transition from *Book 2* of the series. An optional open-ended activity, **Connecting**, encourages students to develop computer skills by searching the Internet for information related to unit themes. Additionally, the appendix includes irregular verb forms, a table of verbs that follow infinitives or gerunds, and a master vocabulary list. An index allows teachers to locate skills found in state standards and on tests.

Composition Practice, Book 3, Third Edition, contains ten units, each providing at least five hours of instructional time. Since students and their teachers can choose among activities offered in a unit, each lesson can either expand to provide more writing practice, or shrink to serve the needs of students in an abbreviated English program.

Each unit is built around a short text. The text, presented as a reading, serves as a means of immersing students in a brief but complete treatment of a high-interest topic. The text also exposes students to new language, provides content for language work, and above all, provides a context for discussion and writing.

At the heart of each lesson are workshop-oriented writing sessions, where students are encouraged to share information and ideas with their classmates. Students are required to view personal experience with an analytic eye and to draw on it to support abstract concepts and assertions. This is one of the most important steps that student writers take in *Composition Practice, Book 3*—they move away from their beginning-level base of relating personal experience toward academic/analytic writing, using their experiences as support.

I wish to acknowledge my former colleagues of the English Language Institute at Central YMCA Community College in Chicago. With them I began the work that led to the *Composition Practice* series. Although the school no longer exists, it was an exciting place and time to teach and learn. I would like to give special thanks to my dear friend, Linda Hillman, who had faith early on that a textbook or two could emerge from my jumble of mimeographed lessons.

I would also like to thank the reviewers, many of whose helpful suggestions were incorporated into this third edition:

Carol Antunano, *English Center,* Miami, FL

Nancy Boyer, *Golden West College,* Huntington Beach, CA

Miguel A. Contreras, *English Language Institute at El Paso* and *El Paso Community College,* El Paso, TX

Jeff DiUglio, *Boston University,* Boston, MA

Terry Paglia, *Newtown High School,* Elmhurst, NY

Kathleen Yearick, *Groves-Wilmington High School,* Wilmington, DE

Contents

To the Teacher

● **The Series**

Composition Practice, Book 3, is an extension of *Books 1* and *2* of the *Composition Practice* series. Like the first two books, its approach is based on a writer's purpose for communicating, whether to inform a reader, share a worthwhile experience, influence a course of action, or analyze a problem. To achieve these purposes, students are trained in an array of strategies available to them as writers of English. The lessons also highlight areas of mechanics, grammar, and cohesion. Finally, like the rest of the series, each unit culminates in writing—the student's own—that reflects and integrates the teaching of the unit.

● **New in *Composition Practice, Book 3***

Book 3 marks a turning point in the *Composition Practice* series. More than *Books 1* and *2,* it gets students to use academic language of the sort needed in their future schoolwork and professional careers. More of the texts in *Book 3,* both those students read and those they write, are analytic. The overall purpose is to nudge students from their initial writing base of relating personal experience toward more public academic writing that analyzes life experience and calls on it to serve in support of broader claims. As mentioned in the Preface (p. iii), the language level of these texts has been simplified somewhat to allow for a smoother transition from *Book 2* of the series.

A second difference is that *Book 3* relies more on formal visual-textual correspondences. Diagrams, maps, charts, and graphs are used throughout the units. Outlining also serves as a means of extracting information and organizing it according to intrinsic logical and semantic relationships.

A third new focus is developing academic skills. Skills such as analyzing, generalizing, inferring, and synthesizing are crucial to the development of proficient and sophisticated readers and writers. Those planning to continue their academic work through the medium of English must begin to articulate their own ideas, while accounting for information and ideas from a multitude of sources—which they begin to do in *Book 3.*

Finally, *Book 3* directs students' attention to greater complexities of the writing process and a writer's responsibilities—reaching an audience, developing a thesis around which a text coheres, collaborating with others, and continually revising for greater clarity and thoroughness.

● Organization of *Composition Practice, Book 3*

Composition Practice, Book 3, comprises ten units, each built around a reading. Preceding each reading, visuals help students establish a context and anticipate the subject area in which they will read. Following each reading, students work with key vocabulary and information that they need to search for in the text.

Next come exercises on mechanical, grammatical, organizational, rhetorical, or cognitive points related to the reading. Most of these exercises can be completed in collaboration and checked orally.

Notes and questions on the reading follow the exercises and are included to help students analyze the reading as a text written by a real person, using rhetorical strategies that they can use in their own writing. In the new edition, this guided questioning—intended for oral discussion—has been moved to the end of the unit to allow more time for students to work with the text as readers before analyzing it from a writer's perspective.

Preliminary writing activities provide students more writing "space" before venturing into "fuller" compositions. Teachers are encouraged to view these activities as practice and experimentation to be entered into notebooks or journals without grades or corrections. When possible, writing should be shared.

Each unit ends with instructions and suggested topics for student compositions. As much collaboration as possible needs to be built into the drafting process, and students should be encouraged to work with partners, who will serve as readers, editors, and friendly critics.

A final activity, **Connecting,** is optional and is designed for students with access to computers. It encourages students to search the Internet for information related to unit themes. They can then either share the information with other classmates or incorporate it into their own compositions.

● Rationale for Certain Aspects of *Composition Practice, Book 3*

The readings in *Composition Practice, Book 3,* are not presented as models for student writers to imitate. While students are required to look at these texts from a writer's perspective in the **Notes and Questions** section of each unit, they are otherwise required to respond as readers, working within the context of the reading without being required to "learn the text," or even comprehend every aspect of it.

Students must be encouraged to look within their own experience and knowledge for connections to each reading. The articulation of that connection, both orally and in writing, is more important than the particulars of a printed text. Teachers need to spend more time plumbing the reactions of students as readers than worrying about whether every line of a text can be explained by students as "proof" of their comprehension.

● A View of Discourse

It may be helpful to examine briefly a traditional view of discourse. Although not all writers agree, discourse is often classified into four major types:

1. Narration
2. Description
3. Argumentation or persuasion
4. Exposition

In brief, a narrative relates a sequence of events; it tells a story. A description describes a process, an object or person, or the way something works. Argumentation tries to persuade or convince. Exposition sets out to explain in some way; it might define, analyze, classify, interpret, or evaluate.

In actuality, no text is exclusively of one type or another. A piece of writing classified as a narrative, for example, could easily include some description, a little exposition, and a bit of argumentation. For teaching purposes, we often separate the types; this is an artificial division, but a pedagogically defensible one when a text is viewed according to the writer's perceived purpose.

Even when various parts of a text can be analyzed and identified differently, it is usually fairly easy to figure out the writer's overall intent. It is this intent that is the basis for the classification specified at the beginning of each unit in *Composition Practice, Book 3*. The tools and techniques that a particular discourse provides for a writer and that discourse's conventions for writing usually make a writer's purpose clear to a reader. It is not a secret that writers should keep to themselves if effective communication is to take place.

● Discourse and *Composition Practice, Book 3*

A correspondence between the four-part classification of discourse above and the units of *Composition Practice, Book 3,* can easily be made.

Discourse type	*Composition Practice, Book 3*
1. narration	none
2. description	Units 1, 2, 7, 8
3. argumentation	Unit 6
4. exposition	Units 3, 4, 5, 9, 10

The terminology used here in the discussion of discourse, at the beginning of the unit, in the **Notes and Questions** in the units, and in the exercise headings may be of help in a teacher's assessment and understanding of the lessons. However, please note that when terms such as *exposition* or *partition* are used in the classroom, they serve as shortcuts in direction-giving or as convenient labels in textual analysis, at best, and should never be mistaken for teaching tools. What is important is that students become proficient writers, whether or not they know or remember the terminology for the various forms, devices, techniques, or patterns they learn to use. To downplay the terms is not, however, to minimalize the importance of training students to understand the concepts and usage for which the terms are only convenient labels.

● **Lesson Plans for Each Unit**

Each unit in *Composition Practice, Book 3,* is designed to provide material for four to five hours of class work. Students enrolled in an intensive English program who meet for composition on an average of five times a week could then complete a unit per week. For these students, the plan for the week might be as follows:

Pre-first class
Students are guided through the visuals at the beginning of each unit, with a brief discussion stimulating interest in the topic of the reading and establishing a context for subsequent work. The actual reading of the text is assigned as homework.

First class
Students are encouraged to comment on the reading, ask questions about content or language, and relate connected experience. Students collaborate on the map work, vocabulary lists, vocabulary exercise, and note-taking. Their work is checked orally, written on the board, or checked individually as the teacher circulates in the room. Students are assigned some or all of the exercises for the next class.

Second class

The exercises assigned as homework are checked orally, or some students write their work on the board. Any unassigned exercises are assigned and checked. Students are assigned a re-reading of the text as homework.

Third class

The teacher guides students through the notes and questions on the reading, keeping the discussion free-flowing and lively. If students notice additional aspects of the reading, they should be encouraged to offer their comments and ask new questions. Some preliminary writing activities are completed in class; others are assigned as homework.

Fourth class

Students share some of their preliminary writing and begin to prepare for their compositions—going over instructions, making decisions on topics, and collaborating with classmates as they brainstorm, make notes, draft, and revise. The atmosphere in the classroom should be that of a workshop, with students moving about freely and quietly helping each other as listeners, readers, editors, and friendly critics. The teacher circulates, serving as a resource. Students can continue work on their compositions as homework. (Perhaps siblings, spouses, roommates, or co-workers could serve as collaborators.) If students have access to computers, they may want to use the **Connecting** activity to search the Internet for additional material for their compositions.

Fifth class

The workshop of the fourth day continues as students further revise, developing their writing into a "final" draft before the class is over. After proofing and making last-minute changes, students give their drafts to each other to read. At the end of the class, students are directed to turn in their compositions or add them to their portfolios. (Even if turned in, the compositions should find their way back to students' portfolios eventually.)

If students meet fewer than five hours a week for composition, more of the middle matter in each unit will need to be assigned as homework or left out altogether. Above all, teachers must preserve class time for students to interact as readers and writers. Students responding to a text and workshop-oriented writing sessions lie at the heart of each unit.

● Evaluation of Student Writing

Teachers are encouraged to read and respond to their students' writing, rather than correct and grade it. Feedback is best provided in the form of written response or, better yet, in individual conferences. If grades are necessary, they should be given on compositions selected for this purpose by students from their own portfolios. Another way to avoid having grades and corrections kill students' desire to take risks, experiment, and thereby make progress is to give periodic composition exams, rather than to grade students' daily or weekly writing.

We teachers, as writers, know that most writing is never really finished: we either run out of time, lose interest, or reach a plateau where a particular text is the best we can make it for the time being. With that in mind, student writers should be encouraged to return to their portfolios periodically to pull out a piece of writing that they feel inspired to work on again. Every piece of writing is then viewed as a work-in-progress; a teacher's system of evaluation should not prohibit this kind of revision.

To the Student

- Welcome to *Composition Practice, Book 3*

Your English is better now, and you are moving closer to being a good writer. Soon, you will be ready to study for an academic degree or do your professional work...*in English*!! Therefore, you must begin to think very carefully about your writing.

In order to get ready for your future studies and work, you must now begin to practice writing a more formal kind of English. This is the kind you will find in college textbooks and in business communication. In your earlier composition classes, you probably wrote only about your daily life. Now, you need to begin to write more about the world around you. For example, you will write about topics from areas such as medicine, economics, and education.

- **Thinking in English**

Now, you must begin to think more *in English*. Try hard not to translate what you want to say or write. You will not be a good writer if you continue to translate everything. As you begin to think more in English, you will need to learn to think in these ways:

1. You must learn to **analyze** in English.

   Example: You might study the PROBLEM of air pollution.

   ⬇

   You look for CAUSES:
   1. automobiles
   2. factory smoke
   3. etc.

2. You must learn to **generalize** in English.

   Example: You might know these FACTS:
   1998: 50 students in the English program
   1999: 75 students in the English program
   2000: 99 students in the English program

   ⬇

   You GENERALIZE
   The program is growing.

3. You must learn to **support with examples.**

Example: You might know a GENERAL TRUTH:
Air has weight.
↓
You use an EXPERIMENT TO PROVE IT:
1. Weigh a flat tire.
2. Fill the tire with air.
3. Weigh the tire again.
4. Compare the difference.

4. You must learn to **synthesize.**

Example: In one book, you might READ:
Picasso was born in 1881.
Picasso lived in France for a
long time.
↓
In another book, you might READ:
Picasso was born in Spain.
Picasso died in France.
↓
In a report on Picasso, you PULL THE FACTS
TOGETHER:
Picasso was born in Spain in
1881 and lived in France
until he died.

● Reason for Writing

In the future, you will have many reasons for writing something. You might be in a chemistry class, for example, and need to answer a question on a final examination. You might be in an office, and need to write a business letter. You might find that you need to answer questions such as these:

1. How does X look?
2. What do we know about X?
3. What do we need to communicate about X?
4. How is X different from Y?
5. How can X be proved?
6. What should be done about X?
7. What is different about X?
8. What series of events led to X?

9. What does X mean?
10. What caused X? What are its consequences? Why is it a problem?

In *Composition Practice, Book 3,* you will learn how to answer such questions. This is what you will do.

To answer the question:	*You will learn to:*
1. How does X look?	describe
2. What do we know about X?	describe and relate
3. What about X needs to be communicated?	communicate by letter
4. How is X different from Y?	contrast
5. How can X be proved?	illustrate
6. What should be done about X?	argue a point
7. What is different about X?	describe and relate
8. What led to X?	describe processes and procedures
9. What does X mean?	define
10. Why is X a problem?	analyze cause and effect

In each unit, you will study how writers of English typically answer these questions. You will then answer such questions yourself.

● **The Plan of Study**

Look at the Table of Contents at the beginning of this book. Notice that in each unit, you will learn to write for a certain purpose; you will learn to write in order to answer certain kinds of questions. You will answer those questions for the reader.

The activities in each unit will follow a certain order. First, you will read something. The reading will show you how a writer can write with a certain purpose in mind. Later, the reading will provide a context for your own composition. After you read and study each reading, you will work with information from the reading. Then, you will do exercises to help you write better. After you complete the exercises, you will go back to the reading and analyze it. This will help you understand how the writer composed the reading. Next, you will do short writing activities to warm you up for more extended writing. Finally, you will plan your composition and write.

Your Compositions

Materials needed

- 8 1/2 x 11 lined notebook paper
- monolingual (English-English) dictionary
- translation dictionary

Planning Before you can begin to write a composition, you must do some careful thinking and planning. First, choose your topic. Second, decide what you want to do with your topic. For example, do you want to describe it? Do you want to define it or analyze it?

Clear Topic Sentences As you begin to write, be sure to tell the reader what you are writing about. Tell the reader indirectly. For example, you would not want to begin your composition this way: *I am going to tell you about air pollution.* Instead, you might want to begin this way: *Air pollution is a major problem in cities today.* Always make the topic clear in the first two or three sentences.

Transitions You should pay careful attention to the movement from one point to another. You might rearrange the word order of a sentence to make the movement smoother. Also, you might add connectors, such as *therefore, however,* or *furthermore,* to allow the reader to move smoothly through your writing.

Editing and Proofreading Be sure to reread your composition several times after you finish writing. Ask yourself if your composition says what you want it to say. Will the reader understand it? Is the grammar correct? Are the words spelled correctly?

Neatness Be sure that your composition looks good. The margins must be clean and neat. Your writing paper should be of standard size. Your work should have a title. Your handwriting should be neat and easy to read. The appearance of your work is very important. You should always take pride in your work.

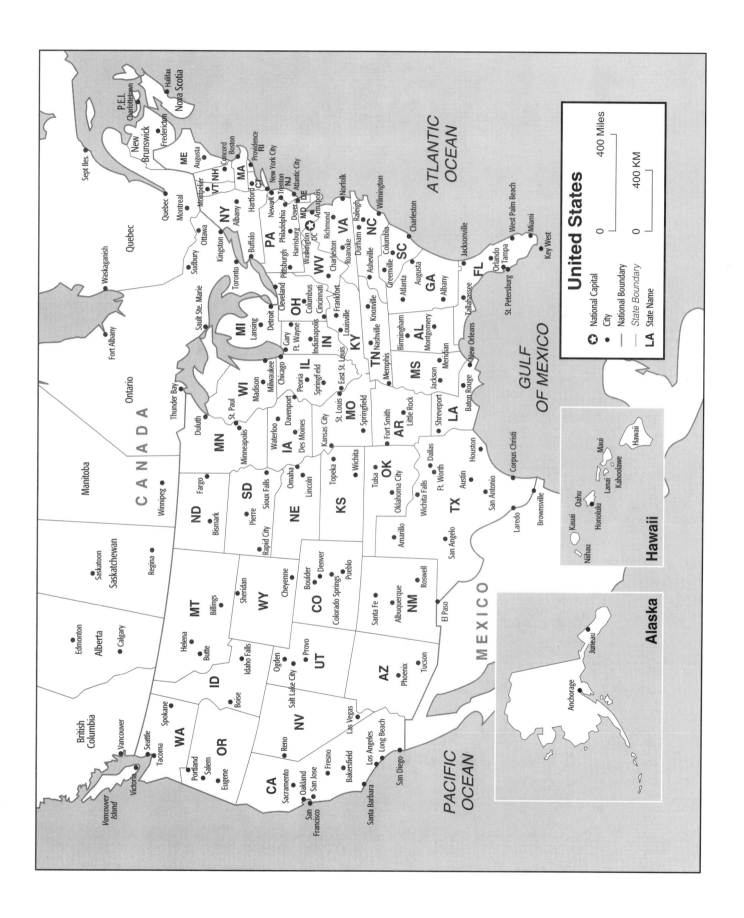

Unit 1 Describing a Place

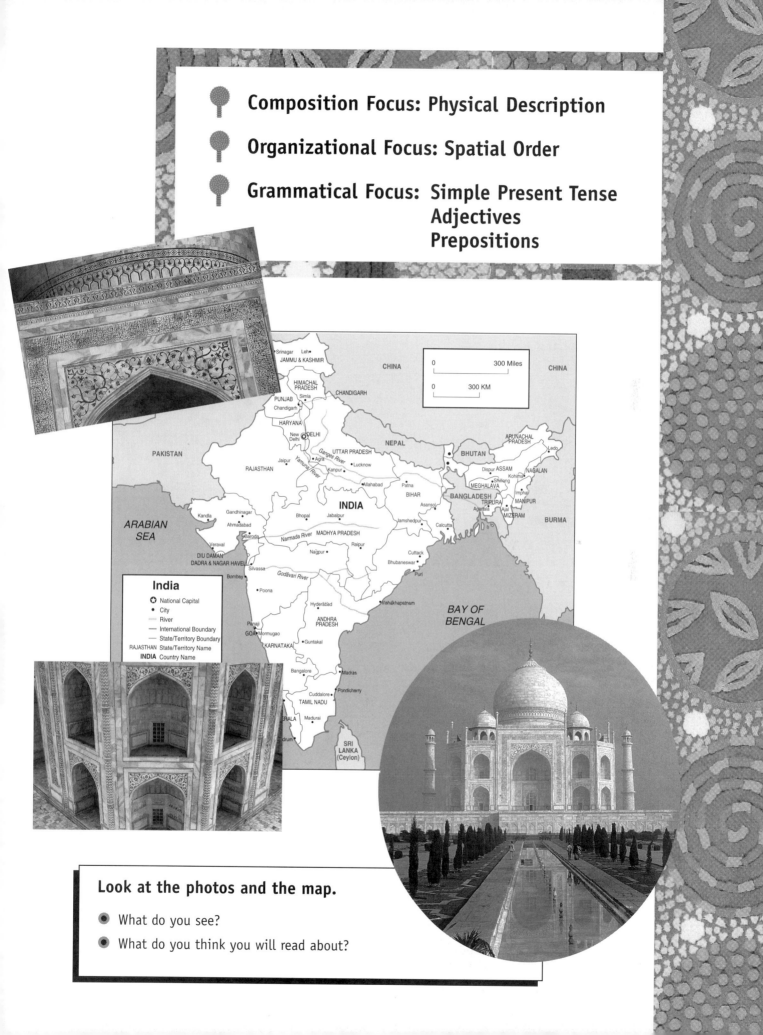

Composition Focus: Physical Description

Organizational Focus: Spatial Order

Grammatical Focus: Simple Present Tense
Adjectives
Prepositions

Look at the photos and the map.

- What do you see?
- What do you think you will read about?

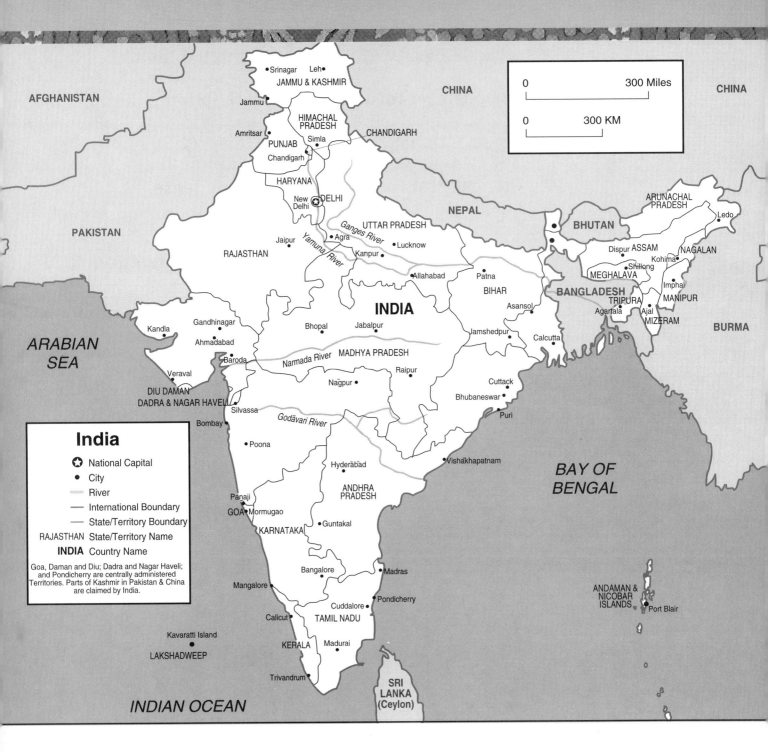

India

★ National Capital
● City
River
International Boundary
State/Territory Boundary
RAJASTHAN State/Territory Name
INDIA Country Name

Goa, Daman and Diu; Dadra and Nagar Haveli;
and Pondicherry are centrally administered
Territories. Parts of Kashmir in Pakistan & China
are claimed by India.

Map Work

1. Locate Agra. Where is it?
2. What countries have a border with India? Where are they?
3. What bodies of water are around India? Where are they?
4. Where is Delhi, India? Where is the island of Sri Lanka?
5. Make up questions that your classmates can answer about this map.

Reading 1

The Taj Mahal

(1) Shah Jahan finished building the Taj Mahal in 1648. He was a rich and powerful emperor, and he built the Taj Mahal as a memorial for his wife. It was a monument of love. The word "taj" means crown. "Mahal" was the name of his wife. Twenty thousand people worked for 18 years to complete this beautiful domed building. A thousand elephants carried huge stones and jewels from all over India and central Asia for the Taj. Shah Jahan wanted this memorial to be a special place for Muslim pilgrims to visit. In addition, he wanted it to be a burial place for himself and his wife.

(2) The Taj Mahal is on the Yamuna River in Agra in northern India. (See the map on page 4.) To many people around the world, the Taj Mahal is a symbol of India. Its picture is in most travel books and brochures. It is open daily from sunrise to sunset. For about fifteen rupees (or about US$.33), anyone can enter this peaceful and quiet place.

(3) As you enter, you pass through beautiful, silent gardens. From the gardens, you cross a wide courtyard. Suddenly, you see the dome of the main building through a tall, red sandstone gate. From the cool, dark gate, the Taj Mahal seems to float between earth and sky. At daybreak, its white walls glow rose. At noon, they blaze white. At dusk, they become dark gray. The Taj Mahal is most beautiful by the light of the full moon. Ah, then you can feel the romance and mystery of the Taj Mahal!

(4) After you pass through the gate, you step onto a wide stone platform. You look over another garden with pools. Everything is arranged carefully in fours. Four is a special number in the Moslem religion. The garden is divided into four parts. There are straight rows of colorful flowers and trees in each of the parts. At the four corners of the Taj Mahal, there are pointed minarets, or tall towers. After the gardens, you go down stone steps towards the main building with the tomb and graves of Shah Jahan and his wife.

(5) After hundreds of years, the Taj Mahal remains a lovely and peaceful place. An inscription at the entrance gate describes the Taj Mahal as "a palace of pearls where the pious can live forever." This beautiful building is truly a jewel for all people.

Vocabulary from Reading 1

Find these words in Reading 1. Examine the use of each word and guess its meaning. If you are not sure, ask a classmate or check your dictionary.

Nouns	Verbs	Adjectives
courtyard	arrange	burial
daybreak	blaze	domed
dome	float	peaceful
dusk	glow	pious
emperor	remain	silent
gate		
grave		
inscription		
jewel		
memorial		
minaret		
mystery		
palace		
pilgrim		
platform		
romance		
sunrise		
sunset		
tomb		

Vocabulary Work

Part A

Use words from the vocabulary list on page 6 to fill in the blanks.

Many tourists to India visit the Taj Mahal. The building is like a

diamond or precious _____ on the banks of the river.

Visitors read the old _____, the words written on the

wall of the entrance _____. They walk through gardens

that someone had carefully planned and _____. The

plants and trees are in perfect lines. Visitors can _____ in

the Taj Mahal all day and enjoy its beauty. The _____

Shah Jahan built a lasting treasure to show his great love for his wife.

Part B

Answer these questions using the vocabulary list on page 6. Work in teams of two or three. (NOTE: Some questions ask for words from the list. Other questions use the words.)

1. Who rules an empire?
2. What is the word for a place built to remember a person?
3. Who takes a long religious trip?
4. Which words mean *the beginning of daylight*?
5. Which words mean *the end of daylight*?
6. Where is a dead body placed?
7. What is a puzzle or question without an answer?
8. What is a large, round part of a building?
9. What type of tower is tall and pointed?
10. Which words are things that glow?

Make up other questions about the words on the list to ask your partner(s).

Taking Notes

Start at the bottom of this diagram and "walk" up. Label each part of the Taj Mahal complex according to the information in Reading 1.

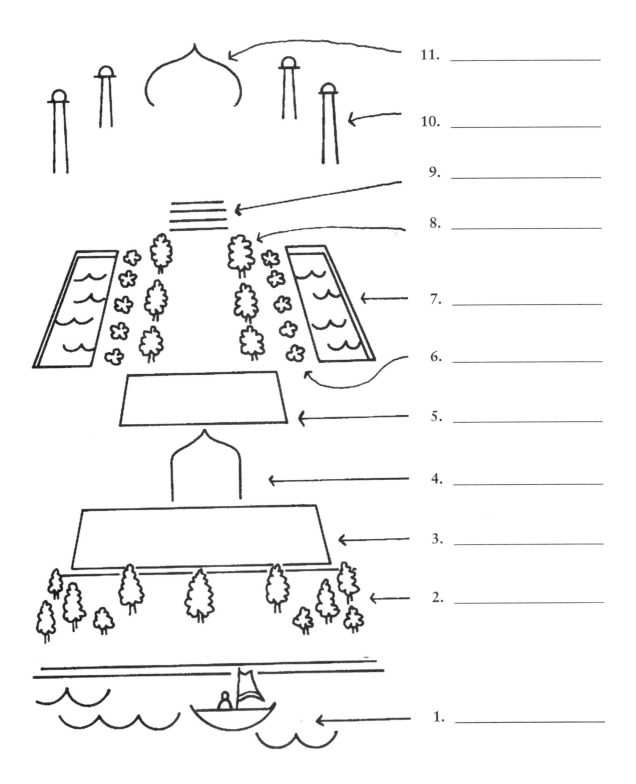

11. _____

10. _____

9. _____

8. _____

7. _____

6. _____

5. _____

4. _____

3. _____

2. _____

1. _____

Exercise A: Using Descriptive Adjectives

Write sentences about the Taj Mahal and its grounds. Use the adjectives below. Use each word only once.

lovely   colorful   peaceful   tall
wide   straight   quiet   pointed
beautiful   silent   special

Example: Tell about the gardens.
             The gardens look lovely. OR *There are lovely gardens.*

1. Tell about the courtyard.

   _____

2. Tell about the walls.

   _____

3. Tell about the Taj Mahal by the light of a full moon.

   _____

4. Tell about the pools.

   _____

5. Tell about the flowers.

   _____

6. Tell about the rows of trees.

   _____

7. Tell about the minarets.

   _____

8. Describe the Taj Mahal.

   _____

Exercise B: Creating a Sense

Close your eyes and imagine each place or scene below. What do you see? What do you hear? What do you smell? What do you feel? List at least three descriptive words for each place or scene below. Choose words to create a special sense or feeling. Use your dictionary to look up words that you need.

1. the Taj Mahal

   _____

2. a mountain lake at sunrise

   _____

3. a jungle full of wild animals

   _____

4. an erupting volcano

   _____

5. a big city at rush hour

   _____

6. a candlelight dinner for two

   _____

Exercise C: Using Prepositions

Complete the sentences below with the following prepositions.

at	*for*	*of*	*to*
between	*from*	*on*	*with*
by	*in*	*through*	

1. The Taj Mahal is _____ the Yamuna River.

2. It is located _____ Agra, India.

3. Thousands of people worked _____ many years to build the Taj Mahal.

4. The monument is open _____ 8:00 _____ 6:00.

5. Visitors walk _____ the tall gate.

6. There is a large garden _____ two pools.

7. There are rows _____ flowers and trees.

8. The tall, round dome is _____ the towers.

9. There are tall towers _____ the corners of the Taj Mahal.

10. Many visitors like to see the building _____ the light of the moon.

Exercise D: Inferring Meaning

Use your understanding of Reading 1 to respond to the following questions. Use your own words to answer. Find information from the reading to support and explain your opinions. Write at least three sentences for each question.

1. How do you think Shah Jahan felt about his wife?

2. Why do you think it took so long to build the Taj Mahal?

3. Why do you think visitors to the Taj Mahal must enter from a distance and pass through quiet gardens and wide courtyards?

Notes and Questions on Reading 1

Part A: Paragraphs

Reading 1 describes a place, the Taj Mahal. The reading selection describes the physical layout. It tells how the place looks and "feels." It gives you, the reader, a "sense" of place. Go back to Reading 1 and underline words that create a sense of place—words that make you feel you are there.

    Example: ...anyone can enter this <u>peaceful</u> and <u>quiet</u> place.

Next, look at the paragraphs. What did the writer describe in each of the paragraphs? Why did the writer divide the reading into the different paragraphs? The following questions may help.

1. How does the writer introduce the subject, Taj Mahal? Why do you think the writer does it that way? What are other ways to introduce this subject?

2. What change is there between the first and second paragraphs? What is the difference in tense and time? In content?

3. In which paragraphs does the writer describe the building? These paragraphs are the body of the selection.

4. How does the writer conclude or end? Why did the writer use that conclusion? Does it bring the reader back to the information in the introduction? What are other ways to conclude a description of the Taj Mahal?

Part B: Order

You probably understand the order of the information in the writer's description of the Taj Mahal and its grounds. Check to make sure by answering the following questions:

1. In the second paragraph, where does the physical description begin? At the site or location? Why or why not?

2. How far does the writer "go" in the third paragraph? (Example: to the entrance? To the gardens?) How far in the fourth paragraph? How far in the fifth paragraph?

3. What is the order of progression through these main paragraphs? (Why isn't the information in the fourth paragraph placed before the information in the third paragraph, etc.?)

4. Look for the words that move the reader through space...through the Taj Mahal. Make a list of words that show space relationships.

5. Turn to the diagram on page 8. Match the parts of the diagram to the paragraphs of the reading.

Reading 1 follows the order of space ("spatial" order) in moving the reader from the entrance of the Taj Mahal to the tomb itself. You will probably use this same kind of order in writing about any physical space.

Preliminary Writing

You and your teacher can decide which of the following activities to do. Write in your journal or in your notebook.

1. Imagine that you are building a memorial to someone you love. Describe it in great detail. Draw a plan or picture to illustrate your description.

2. Choose a place or a scene from Exercise B on page 8. Use your list of words from Exercise B to build a paragraph. Be sure to create a particular sense. (Let your classmates decide if you are successful!)

3. The information below is not in Reading 1. Rewrite Reading 1 and add the new information in your own words. Make changes as you go.
    *   Mumtaz Mahal died while bearing the Shah's fourteenth child.
    *   A red sandstone mosque stands to the left of the Taj Mahal. It is full of Moslem pilgrims every Friday.
    *   The Shah's chief architect, Master Ahmed of Lahore, was probably responsible for the Taj Mahal's design. Nobody knows for sure.

4. Describe a place from your childhood. Describe it in such detail that your classmates can draw a sketch or diagram of it from your description.

5. Go back to the diagram on page 8. "Walk" a visitor through the Taj Mahal complex. From your sentences, a reader should understand the layout and the beauty and peaceful feeling of the place.

Composition 1 (Physical Description)

Instructions for Composition 1

Please follow the instructions below. Work in pairs whenever possible, especially with numbers 3, 4, 8, and 9.

1. Think of a place that you want to describe. It must be a place that has meaning to you and to other people who go there. If you need ideas, some topics are suggested on page 15. Choose a topic appropriate for a travel magazine.

2. Draw a sketch, diagram, or plan of the place. This will help you to begin thinking about the layout.

3. Close your eyes and imagine you are at the place. Make a list of adjectives to describe the place. Look over the list. Is there a pattern or theme to the words on your list?

4. Decide on a theme or a sense that you want to create. Is your place peaceful? Sad? Is it a place of romance? Mystery? Add more words to your list that help carry your theme. Keep in mind the readers of travel magazines. You will want to persuade them to visit the place.

5. Start drafting (writing) with phrases and sentences that come to mind.

6. Go back to Reading 1, if you wish, and use it as a model for ideas, vocabulary, and grammar.

7. Write a full draft of your composition. Read it to yourself and see what changes you want to make. Make changes as you go.

8. Check your draft against these questions:

    • Does your introduction make the reader want to continue reading?

    • Is your description complete and orderly? (Can the reader follow easily?)

    • What feeling or sense do you create?

    • Do you have enough descriptive words to create a sense or feeling? Will your description persuade your reader to visit the place?

    • Is your conclusion interesting? Does it give more information or understanding to the reader?

9. Exchange drafts with a partner. Help each other by asking questions or giving suggestions. Write a second draft, if necessary.

10. Proofread your essay before you turn it in or share it with others. Check the following:
   - Do you have a title?
   - Do you have margins?
   - Did you divide your essay into paragraphs?
   - Did you indent the first word of each paragraph?

Also, check capital letters, punctuation, and spelling. If appropriate, give the reader of your composition a picture or drawing of the place you describe.

The Jefferson Memorial in Washington, D.C., U.S.A.

Suggested Topics for Composition 1

Write about:

1. the Kaaba in Mecca, Saudi Arabia
2. Stonehenge in Wiltshire County, England
3. the Eiffel Tower in Paris, France
4. Lake Victoria in east central Africa
5. Machu Picchu in the Andes of Peru
6. Angkor Wat in Angkor, Cambodia
7. the Parthenon in Athens, Greece
8. the Grand Canyon in Arizona, U.S.A.
9. the Jefferson Memorial in Washington, D.C., U.S.A. (see p. 14)
10. Chichén Itzá in the Yucatán, Mexico
11. a temple, shrine, or other holy place that you have visited
12. a place that is famous in the history of your hometown or home country
13. a place that is extremely odd in some way
14. a place that is significant in your life but is not well known to others

Note: Actual pictures of numbers 1–10 above may be found in encyclopedias, *National Geographic,* and other publications. Add pictures or your own drawings to illustrate your composition.

 # Connecting

Search the Internet for information, photos, or diagrams of your place. Use the information you find in your composition or share the information with a partner.

Unit 2 Portraying a Person

- **Composition Focus:** Biography

- **Organizational Focus:** Chronological Order

- **Grammatical Focus:** Simple Past Tense
  Past Continuous Tense

Look at the photos and the map. Describe what you see to a classmate.

- What do you think you will read about?
- What do you know about this place?

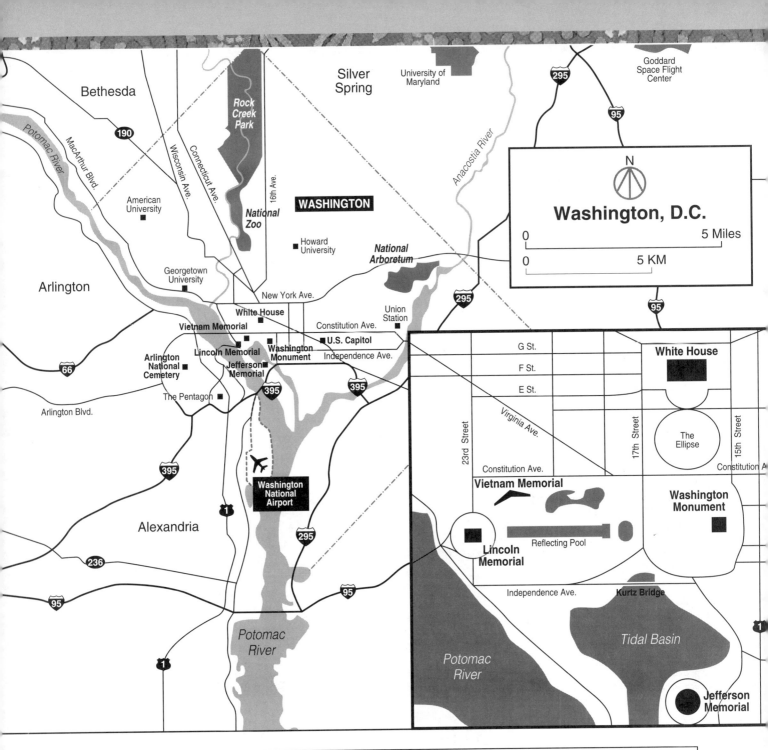

Map Work

1. Locate the Vietnam Memorial. Where is it?

2. Locate the White House. Where is it in relationship to the Vietnam Memorial?

3. Locate the Washington Monument. Where is it in relationship to the Vietnam Memorial?

4. What river borders Washington, D.C.? Where is the U.S. Capitol? Where is Arlington National Cemetery?

5. Make up questions to ask your classmates about this map.

Reading 2

The Unknown Architect

(1) In April 1981, a group of people met in Washington, D.C. They had to choose a design for the Vietnam Memorial. There were 1,421 entries in the contest. After four days, the group finally chose a winner. The winning design was number 1,026. But who was the designer of 1,026? It was probably a professional architect, right? No, it wasn't. It was a college student named Maya Ying Lin. (See page 20.)

(2) At the time, Maya Lin, a young Asian-American woman, was studying at Yale University in New Haven, Connecticut. She was taking an architecture class. Her professor gave the class a homework assignment to design a war memorial. Maya Lin thought about the assignment carefully and prepared her design. Her professor looked at it. He thought it was too strong, but he wanted her to enter the contest. Maya Lin didn't expect to win. She thought her design was too simple.

(3) In Maya Lin's design, there were 3,000 cubic feet of black granite. The granite was cut into 150 panels. These panels rose out of the ground as a V-shaped wall. In her design, the names of all the dead soldiers appeared on the wall. Maya Lin wanted the names to appear in the order of the day they died. A visitor would read the wall like a poem.

(4) Maya Lin did not want the memorial to be cold or distant. She wanted people to touch it, feel it, and mostly to experience it. She wanted to honor the men and women who lost their lives in the Vietnam War.

(5) Maya Lin chose black granite because it seemed peaceful and reflective. She wanted the stone to rise from the earth like a line between the world of the living and the quiet, dark world beyond. For the inscription, she used the names of the dead soldiers.

(6) When Maya Lin saw the memorial for the first time, she felt afraid. It seemed strange to see her personal and private idea out in public. Maya Lin came to the memorial another time as a visitor. She watched as people touched names on the wall and remembered friends and relatives. Some of the people left flowers, photos, and personal items near the wall. Later, as Maya Lin was walking beside the wall, she found the name of a friend's father. She touched the name and cried. She reacted to the memorial the same way that so many other visitors do.

(7) Maya Lin continued to design monuments until 1989. At that time, she wanted to do more with art and architecture. She said, "When I was 21 years old, I was labeled 'architect' because I was an architecture student when I did the Vietnam Memorial. I want to be more of an artist who happens to build architecture." Maya Lin says she is interested in "presenting factual information allowing the viewer the chance to come to his or her own conclusions."

Vocabulary from Reading 2

Find these words in Reading 2. Examine the use of each word and guess its meaning. If you are not sure, ask a classmate or check your dictionary.

Nouns
architect
architecture
contest
cubic feet
design
designer
entry
granite
panel
soldier

Verbs
design
expect
experience
honor
react

Adjectives
distant
peaceful
personal
private
professional
public
reflective

Other
beyond

Maya Ying Lin

Vocabulary Work

Part 1

Match the words below with their meanings.

_____ 1. experience   a. a competition

_____ 2. expect   b. to think something will happen

_____ 3. distant   c. something entered in a contest

_____ 4. personal   d. to plan, draw, or sketch

_____ 5. contest   e. to act after something happens

_____ 6. entry   f. to participate in or do something

_____ 7. soldier   g. for use by the people

_____ 8. react   h. a person who is in an army

_____ 9. design   i. far away

_____ 10. public   j. private; belonging to one person

Part 2

Answer these questions from the vocabulary list on page 20. Work in groups of two or three. (NOTE: Some questions ask for words from the list. Other questions use the words.)

1. Who designs buildings and spaces?

2. What is the field of study for designers of buildings and spaces?

3. What is a type of stone often used for memorials?

4. What word is a *piece* or *section* of a wall?

5. What are we doing when we show respect to the dead?

6. Which word means *marked by quiet and calm*?

Make up other questions about the words on the list to ask your partner(s).

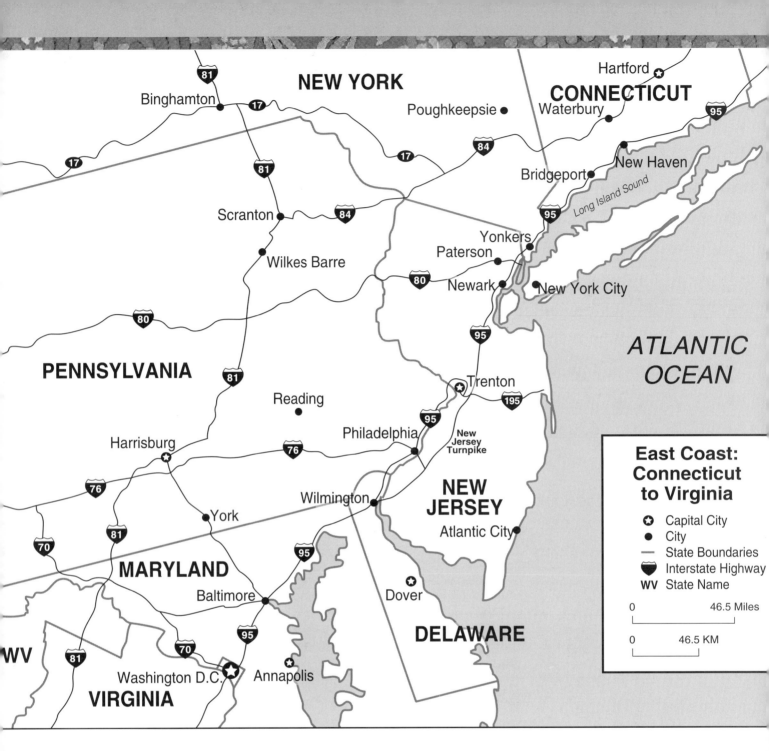

Map Work

1. Locate New Haven, Connecticut. Where is it in relationship to New York City? In relationship to Washington, D.C.? Why is New Haven mentioned in Reading 2?

2. Trace the route from New Haven to Washington, D.C. Tell your classmates how to drive from one city to the other.

3. What major cities are between New York and Washington, D.C.?

4. Ask your classmates questions about the map.

Taking Notes

Please complete the outline below with information from Reading 2.

The Unknown Architect: Maya Ying Lin

I. Background: Lin's design wins

    A. What?

    B. When?

    C. the committee's reaction:

II. Background: Lin before the design contest

    A. student at Yale

    B. reason for design:

    C. reaction to the design:

        1. Lin's professor's reaction:

        2. Lin's reaction:

III. What Lin wanted in a design

    A.

    B.

    C.

    D.

IV. Reasons for Lin's choice

    A. black granite:

    B. stone rising from the ground:

    C. the inscription on the stone:

V. Lin's reaction to the memorial afterward

    A.

    B.

Exercise A: Using Past Tense Verbs

Complete the sentences below with the past tense form of the following verbs. Use each verb only once.

choose   *design*   *meet*   *think*
come   *expect*   *react*   *cry*
honor   *see*

1. Maya Lin never _____ to win the design contest.

2. Maya Lin's professor _____ that her design was too strong. She considered it too simple.

3. The group _____ for four days to discuss the entries and choose the winning design.

4. The group _____ Maya Lin's design over 1,420 others.

5. Maya Lin _____ the stone panels to rise out of the ground.

6. Maya Lin's design _____ the soldiers who died by putting all of their names on the memorial.

7. When Maya Lin _____ the memorial in place for the first time, she was afraid.

8. Many people _____ to the memorial during the first weeks to find the names of their dead friends.

9. Mothers, fathers, husbands, wives, sisters, brothers, sons, and daughters _____ when they found the names of their loved ones.

10. Maya Lin herself _____ to the memorial in the same way that so many other visitors had.

Exercise B: Using Simple Past vs. Past Continuous Tense

The simple past and past continuous tenses often show the relationship between two different actions. The past continuous is used to describe an action that was going on when another action took place and ended.

Write the *simple past* or *past continuous* to complete the sentences.

1. Maya Lin was doing her homework when she _____ (have) a great idea.

2. While she _____ (design) the memorial, she thought of friends and family.

3. When Maya Lin _____ (see) her professor on campus, he was talking to another student.

4. The committee _____ (examine) many different designs while they were judging the contest.

5. While workers _____ (building) the memorial, Maya Lin watched the construction.

6. While Maya Lin _____ (visit) the people at the memorial, she saw the name of a friend's father.

Exercise C: Inferring Meaning

Please discuss the questions below with a partner or group.

1. Why did Maya Lin want the names of the soldiers to appear in the order of the day they died?

2. Why did she want people to touch the names on the granite panels?

3. Why did Maya Lin choose black granite for the memorial?

4. Why did she design the panels to look like they were rising from the ground?

5. Why was Maya Lin afraid when she first saw the memorial?

Notes and Questions on Reading 2

Part A: Paragraphs

Reading 2 tells about a special event in the life of a person. You learn about this person through the event. You learn about what she did and who she is. You know her through her ideas and her reactions. You probably admire and respect her because of what you know. What words describe the kind of person she is? Make a list of at least four words.

_____   _____   _____   _____

Look at the paragraphs in the reading. Try to find the writer's reasons for the divisions between paragraphs. The following questions may help.

1. How does the writer introduce the subject? Why does the writer wait so long to name her?

2. How many paragraphs does the writer take to explain the details of the design?

3. Look at how the writer explains the design. Do you learn about the memorial? Do you also learn about Maya Lin's personality?

4. How does the writer conclude? How effective is the conclusion?

Part B: Order

You probably understand the order of the information in the reading. Check to make sure by answering the following questions.

1. What happened first in time—the events in the first or the second paragraph? Why does the writer use this order?

2. What kind of information does the writer give you in the second and third paragraphs?

3. How is the content of the third and fourth paragraphs connected?

4. How is the sixth paragraph different from the fourth and fifth paragraphs?

5. How is the seventh paragraph connected to the rest of the reading?

Reading 2 basically follows the order of time—chronological order—but time is not the most important information. The subject, Maya Lin, is more important. Time only provides a frame for telling about the subject.

Preliminary Writing

You and your teacher can decide which of the following activities to do. Write in your journal or in your notebook.

1. Write about Maya Lin. Describe her personality from what you know. What do you like best about her? Would you want someone like her as a friend?

2. Create a "future" biography of Maya Lin. Where is she now? What is she doing? What important work has she done? What kind of future do you see for her?

3. Rewrite the first three paragraphs of Reading 2. Rearrange the time. Start with Maya Lin in her architecture class at Yale. Her professor has given her a homework assignment to design a war memorial. Take it from there.

4. Not everyone liked Maya Lin's design. Some people wanted the names of the dead in alphabetical order. Think about this idea. Take the two arrangements—the names in alphabetical order or the names in chronological order by the date each soldier died. What is the different effect on a visitor to the memorial? Explain the importance of the different arrangements.

5. Imagine that you are personally connected to the Vietnam War—either as a soldier who lost a friend or as a relative of someone who died there. You recently visited the Memorial for the first time. Describe what you saw and how you felt. Tell how you reacted. Use your imagination.

Composition 2 (Biography)

Instructions for Composition 2

Please follow the instructions below. Work in pairs whenever possible, especially with numbers 2–5 and 7–8.

1. Think of a person you know. The person does not need to be famous, but it should be someone you admire. (Some ideas are suggested on the next page, if you need some help.) You are going to write a human interest article in a magazine about this person.

2. Make a list of words and phrases that describe this person. Don't stop until you run out of ideas. Look over the list. See if the list includes the most important points about the person. Does your list include *who, what, when, where, why,* and *how?*

3. From your list, choose the words and ideas that you want to include in your composition. Circle them. Think about who is going to read your article.

4. To help organize your ideas, look back at the outline for Reading 2. Make an outline like that one. This will help you find "holes" in your thinking. What more do you need to include?

5. Think about your subject as you look back at your list and your outline. Will the reader get to know your person through your eyes? Will the reader learn more than the simple facts?

6. Write a full draft of your composition. Then read it to yourself and see what changes you want to make.

7. After you make changes, check your draft. Ask these questions:

    • Does your introduction pull the reader in?

    • Does your introduction present your subject to the reader?

    • Do you describe your subject's character and personality?

    • Is your conclusion interesting? Does it add something new?

8. Proofread your composition before you turn it in or share it with others. Check the following:

    • Title, margins, paragraph divisions, indented paragraphs, capital letters, punctuation, and spelling.

If possible, include a picture or sketch of your subject.

Suggested Topics for Composition 2

Write about:

1. A person who saved your life

2. A person who helped your family survive a bad time

3. A person who made an important difference in the lives of the people in your village or hometown

4. The person who liberated your country

5. A person whom you admire and respect

6. A person whose intelligence you admire

7. A person whose creativity you admire

8. A person who educated you and others

9. A person who has influenced your life

10. A person with whom you would like to become friends

11. Your best friend

12. A person whose work (in art, in medicine, in education, etc.) is important, in your opinion

 # Connecting

Search the Internet for information about a memorial or monument in your hometown or country. Share the information you find with a partner.

Unit 3

Informing and Requesting

Look at the model of a business letter on the right.

- Whose address will be in the upper right corner?
- Whose address will be below it to the left?
- In what ways does a business letter look different from a personal letter?

Composition Focus: Business Letter Form

Organizational Focus: Order by Importance

Grammatical Focus: Present Tenses
Complex Sentences

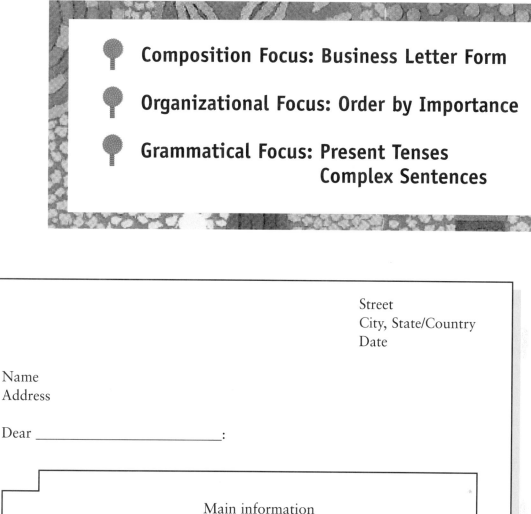

Street
City, State/Country
Date

Name
Address

Dear _____:

Main information

Additional information

Closing remarks

Sincerely,

(signature)

Typed name
Title (if there is one)

Reading 3

I

Please read the following information about Carlos Santoyo before you read his letter.

Biographical Information

(1) Carlos Santoyo came to the United States from Mexico two years ago. Now he is living with his aunt and uncle in Burbank, California. When Carlos was in high school in Mexico City, he studied English and computer science. He also learned some clerical skills while he was working part-time in an office near his home.

(2) After high school, his aunt and uncle invited him to join them in Burbank. They have lived there many years and their own children are grown. They thought Carlos might enjoy the Los Angeles area. At the same time, he could further his education at nearby Glendale Community College.

(3) After Carlos arrived in the Los Angeles area, he got a job as an office assistant for a small company that sells computers and office technology. Now, his aunt and uncle are encouraging him to improve his computer skills by studying data processing at Glendale Community College. Carlos has heard that the college has a good data processing program, and he is eager to start courses.

(4) Carlos would like to get a better-paying job and get on with his life. Although he likes living with his aunt and uncle, he wants to settle down and have his own family someday. He thinks that he will have good employment opportunities in data processing—either in Los Angeles or Mexico City.

II

Business Letter

2539 Olive Avenue
Burbank, CA 91502
April 2, 2001

Glendale Community College
Office of Admissions
1500 North Verdugo Road
Glendale, CA 91208

Dear Admissions Officer:

I am writing to request an application for admission to Glendale Community College for the fall semester, 2001. Please also send information on student loans and financial aid.

At present, I am working as an office assistant. I want to upgrade my skills, and I am especially interested in your program in data processing. I understand that Glendale Community College works with companies to train students for future employment. I would like to take advantage of your job placement services.

Thank you for your assistance. I am eager to further my education at Glendale Community College and improve my job skills.

Sincerely,

Carlos Santoyo

Carlos Santoyo

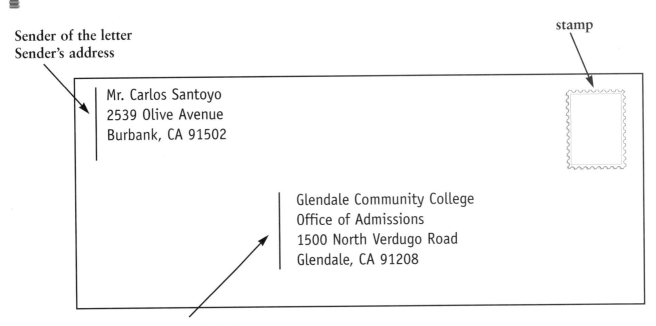

Sender of the letter
Sender's address

Mr. Carlos Santoyo
2539 Olive Avenue
Burbank, CA 91502

stamp

Glendale Community College
Office of Admissions
1500 North Verdugo Road
Glendale, CA 91208

Receiver of the letter
(Receiver can be a company,
an institution, or a person)
Receiver's address

Vocabulary from Reading 3

Find these words in Reading 3. Examine the use of each word and guess
its meaning. If you are not sure, ask a classmate or check your dictionary.

Nouns	Verbs	Adjectives
admission	encourage	better-paying
application	further	clerical
assistance	improve	eager
community college	request	future
computer science	settle down	
data processing	take advantage of	
employment	train	
financial aid	upgrade	
office assistant		
opportunity	**Adverbs**	
placement service	currently	
program	especially	
skills		
student loan		

Vocabulary Work

Part 1

Match the words below with their meanings.

_____ 1. admission

_____ 2. train

_____ 3. clerical

_____ 4. skills

_____ 5. assistance

_____ 6. settle down

_____ 7. data processing

_____ 8. program

_____ 9. take advantage of

a. to begin living an orderly life as an adult

b. a course of study at a school

c. using and analyzing information on a computer

d. to give hope or show support for

e. to put something to good use

f. to prepare someone to do something

g. entry into a school

h. related to office work and keeping records

i. abilities or things a person can do after training or experience

j. help or aid

Part 2

Answer these questions using the vocabulary list on page 34. Work in teams of two or three. (NOTE: Some questions ask for words from the list. Other questions use the words.)

1. A student wants to apply to a school. What form does he or she fill out?

2. If students need money for school, what can they ask for?

3. What does an office assistant do at work?

4. Which word means *work*?

5. What service do schools have to help students find jobs?

6. Which word means *ask*?

7. Which word means *to be or make better*?

8. Which word means *raise to a higher level*?

9. Which word means that someone is ready and willing to do something?

10. Which word means *something is happening now, at this time*?

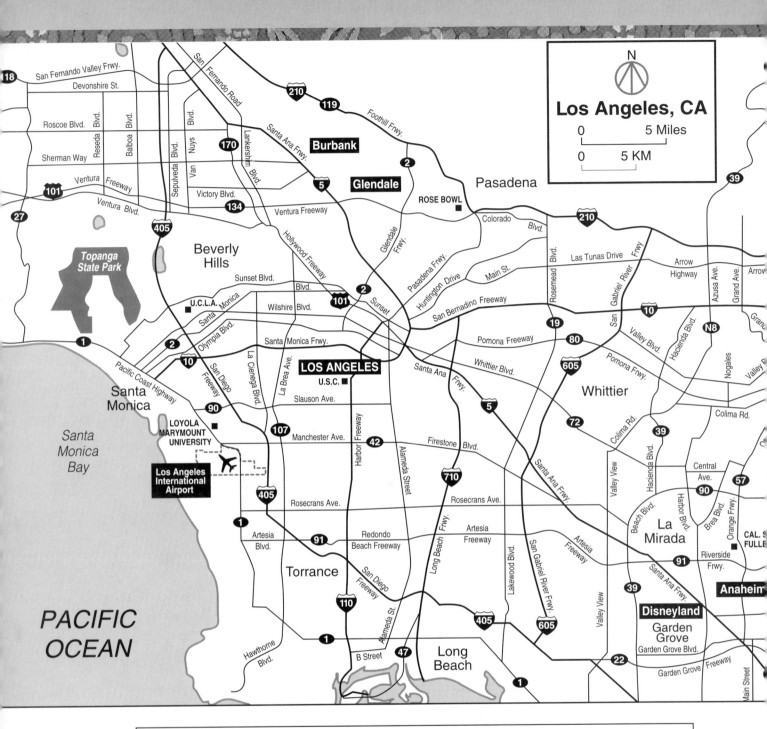

Map Work

1. Where is Glendale in relationship to Burbank? (Remember that Carlos Santoyo lives in Burbank and wants to attend school in Glendale.)

2. Where are Glendale and Burbank in relationship to Los Angeles?

3. Trace a route for Carlos from Burbank to Disneyland in Anaheim. Tell your classmates the route.

4. Find the Los Angeles International Airport. Carlos wants to drive to this airport. How does he get there from Burbank? Explain his route.

5. Ask your classmates questions about the map.

Taking Notes

A business letter is different from a composition, but it still has a clear organization. Please complete the following outline with information from Reading 3.

Carlos Santoyo's Letter

I.   Reasons for writing the letter—what Carlos wants

    A.

    B.

II. Additional information—Carlos's goals at Glendale C.C.

    A.

    B.

III. Closing comments

    A.

    B.

Exercise A: Recognizing Different Styles

Read the following pairs of sentences and phrases. One is more formal and may be used in a business letter. The other is less formal and may be used in a personal letter. Analyze each pair. Write *business* for the one that is formal. Write *personal* for the other.

1. A. Dear John,

   B. Dear Mr. Robertson:

2. A. Love,

   B. Sincerely,

3. A. Thank you for your assistance.

   B. Thanks a lot for helping me.

4. A. I could use some information on loans.

   B. Please send me information on student loans.

5. A. I am eager to further my education at your school.

   B. I really want to go to your school.

6. A. Could you send me an application?

   B. I am writing to request an application.

7. A. Please inform me of your deadline for applications.

   B. Can you tell me your deadline for applications?

8. A. I understand that you offer job placement services.

   B. Somebody told me that you find jobs for people.

9. A. Please help me.

   B. I would appreciate your help.

10. A. Sincerely,

    Carlos Santoyo

    Carlos Santoyo

    B. Your buddy,

    Carlos

Exercise B: Compound Nouns

English speakers sometimes use *noun + noun* to identify something. The second or last noun is what the speaker is talking about. The first noun names something about the other: its location, the material it's made of, its purpose, or the total unit of which it's a part.

Examples: LOCATION (of the head noun): a kitchen table
MATERIAL (from which the head noun is made): a paper cup
PURPOSE (that the head noun serves): a cake pan
TOTAL (of which the head noun is a part): a chair leg

To practice the four relationships above, rewrite each of the following and make a compound noun.

A.

1. a sink that we use in the bathroom _____
2. a stove that we use in the kitchen _____
3. a chair that we use in the living room _____
4. a counter that we have in the kitchen _____
5. a machine that we use in an office _____

B.

1. a chair made of cloth _____
2. a vase made of glass _____
3. a coat made of leather _____
4. a cup made of plastic _____
5. a toy made of rubber _____

C.

1. skills for a job _____
2. a form for an application _____
3. services for job placement _____
4. a loan for tuition _____
5. training for a job _____

D.

1. a leg of a table _____
2. the top of a table _____
3. a seat of a chair _____
4. a cover of a book _____
5. the science of computers _____

Exercise C: Present Tenses

Please write the correct form (simple present tense or present continuous tense) of the verbs in parentheses. Use the simple present tense for habitual repeated activities and general statements of facts. Use the present continuous for activities that are happening right now.

> *Examples:* Right now, Carlos *is living* in Burbank with relatives. (live)
> He *likes* the Los Angles area. (like)

1. Carlos _____ an office assistant job. (have)

2. The company _____ computers and other technology. (sell)

3. Right now, Carlos _____ records and _____ paperwork. (keep, do)

4. He often _____ a computer at work. (use)

5. Many companies in the Los Angeles area _____ employees with data processing skills. (need)

6. The courses at Glendale C.C. _____ students for data processing jobs. (train)

7. Currently, many people _____ their computer skills in community colleges. (upgrade)

8. Carlos's aunt and uncle _____ him apply to Glendale C.C. (help)

9. Most of the colleges _____ financial aid and loans to students. (offer)

10. Glendale C.C. _____ students find jobs after graduation. (help)

Exercise D: Writing Complex Sentences

The following examples use *that, if,* and *after* to combine sentences in special ways:

- We told him that we could not meet the deadline.
- We want to see him if he wants to see us.
- I need to make an appointment after I take my exams.

Interpretation:

- (using *that*) We told him…WHAT INFORMATION?
- (using *if*) We want to see him…UNDER WHAT CONDITIONS?
- (using *after*) I need to make an appointment…WHEN? WHAT COMES FIRST?

Read the pairs of sentences below. Then combine them by using *that, after,* or *if.* Write the combined sentences.

1. We are sorry to tell you. The company is now out of business.

   _____

2. We have decided. We need more time to complete the project.

   _____

3. We hope. You will decide to apply for admission.

   _____

4. We would like to talk to you. You complete your college education.

   _____

5. I am sorry. I was not able to talk to you.

   _____

6. Please write to us. There are further questions.

   _____

7. We would like to inform you. We have received your application.

   _____

8. Please feel free to write to us. We can help you.

   _____

9. Please telephone us. You have arrived.

   _____

10. I am writing to tell you. I have not received my order.

    _____

Notes and Questions on Reading 3

Paragraphs and Order

A business letter is different from a composition. It is usually brief, direct, and very limited in its subject. Basically, the structure is something like this:

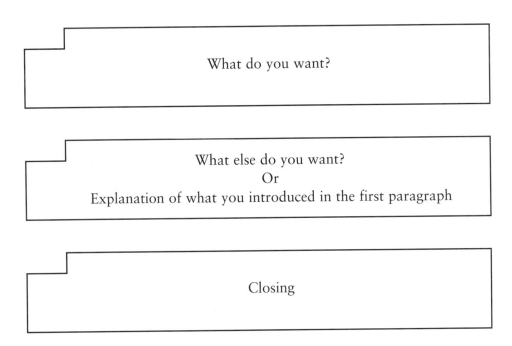

What do you want?

What else do you want?
Or
Explanation of what you introduced in the first paragraph

Closing

If you do not state clearly and precisely what you want in your first paragraph, your letter may go into someone's wastebasket. (Your reader is probably a busy person!)

Go back to the letter at the beginning of Unit 3 to identify this basic structure. If a writer has a lot of business to conduct, a business letter may be longer. It is still always direct and as brief as possible.

The order of a business letter is by importance: the most important points are first, the less important points are next, and the least important points (in terms of new information) are last.

Preliminary Writing

You and your teacher can decide which of the following activities to do. Write in your journal or in your notebook.

1. Make a complete list of all the reasons to write to a school.

2. You ordered something—a jacket, a calculator, an answering machine, etc.—through the mail. When it arrived, something was wrong with it. Now, you want to send it back to the company. Without writing a complete letter, simply state why you are writing and what you want the company to do.

3. Reword the second paragraph of the letter to Glendale Community College on page 33. Since you are not Carlos Santoyo, explain who you are. Explain what you want to do at Glendale C.C. and what services you need from the school. Use your imagination. Change the final paragraph so that it is appropriate for your purposes.

4. Write a brief paragraph about Carlos Santoyo. Who is he? What do you know about him? What is his situation? What are his plans?

5. Write a brief paragraph about Glendale Community College. Where is it? What type of school is it? Who do you think goes there? What programs and services does it offer? Why do you think students go there? Would you go there? (Perhaps your description could appear in a brochure about the school!)

6. Make a list of all the places and people you might ever need to write a business letter to. Also list the reasons for writing For example:

   • Write to a school to ask for an application for admission.
   • Write to a company to complain about a product.

   See how long you can make your list.

Composition 3 (Business Letter Form)

Instructions for Composition 3

Please follow the instructions below. Work in pairs whenever possible, especially with numbers 4 and 7.

1. You will need a definite reason for writing a business letter. Either choose one from the suggested topics on the next page, or think of your own. Decide what supporting information you will need to include. Be brief and to the point.

2. Make some notes before you write.

3. Write your letter from your notes. The basic text of your letter will probably have at least three paragraphs: a reason for writing, additional information, and a closing.

4. Read through your draft to see if it says what you want. Make changes where you want. Then, check your draft against these questions:

   • Do you clearly state why you are writing?

   • Do you add enough supporting information?

   • Do you close your letter politely?

5. Don't give your letter a title. Letters don't need titles. Word-process your letter on a computer, if possible. Use letterhead stationery from your school or company if that is appropriate. If your letter is from you (and not from your school or company), use unlined 8$\frac{1}{2}$ by 11 inch paper.

6. Address a business envelope to go with your letter. Look at the envelope in this unit to see how to address it.

7. Proofread your letter, checking for spelling, punctuation, grammar, capital letters, and proper business form. Then mail it, if appropriate, after you show it to your teacher.

Suggested Topics for Composition 3

1. Write to your utility company (electric, gas, water, telephone, etc.). Explain that you have already paid your bill. (The company is claiming that you haven't paid.) Include the number of your check or money order, your account number with the company, and the date of your payment. Be polite, even if you are frustrated.

2. Write to a college or university to ask for particular information. Tell what you are interested in. If appropriate, tell if you would be a transfer student or a new freshman (first year student).

3. After looking for job information in the classified section of your local newspaper, write to a particular company to apply for a job. Tell where you saw the advertisement. Be precise about the particular job. Tell about your qualifications and your related experience. In other words, "sell" yourself.

4. Write to a city, state, or national agency for tourist information. (You and your teacher can find an address to write to.) Ask for camping information, information on lodging (hotels, etc.), or information on local attractions. If everyone in the class writes to a different agency, you can all share the information you receive.

5. Write a business letter that you really need to write:

   • to a company to complain about a product,

   • to a government agency to ask for a certain piece of information,

   • to a corporation or company to apply for a job.

Take advantage of this assignment to get help writing a letter for a real purpose.

Connecting

Search the Internet for information about the company, government agency, or college that you wrote to in Composition 3. Are there ways to contact them through the Internet? Share the information you find.

Unit 4 Analyzing

Survey

Reasons students give for choosing community colleges

1. lower costs
2. smaller classes
3. more individual attention
4. better teachers
5. job-oriented programs
6. adjustable schedules

- **Composition Focus: Analysis by Contrast**
- **Organizational Focus: Partition**
- **Grammatical Focus: Simple Present Tense Comparatives**

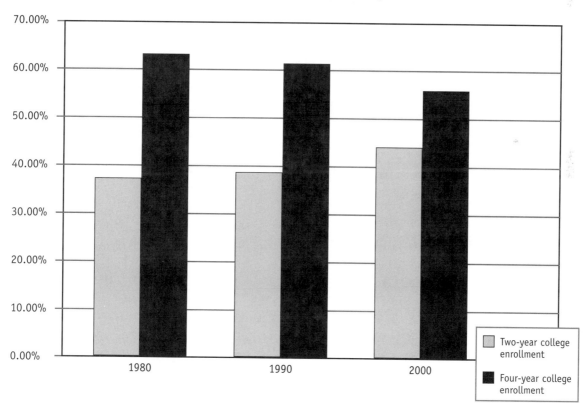

Community colleges gaining popularity
2-year and 4-year colleges by percentage of enrollment

Legend:
- ▢ Two-year college enrollment
- ▮ Four-year college enrollment

Look at the information above.

- What does the graph compare?
- What can you learn from the graph?
- What can you learn from the survey to the left?

Reading 4

U.S. Community Colleges, Enrollment on the Rise

(1) At Houston Community College, in Houston, Texas, students pay $1,296 a year in tuition. At Texas Southern University in Houston, students pay $2,064 in tuition a year. These Texas fees are much lower than in some other parts of the country. But the state of Texas wants every high school student to be able to go to college in the state. It encourages students to begin at a community college for two years and then transfer to a four-year college. As a result, some students are entering community colleges, such as Houston Community College, to save money. But lower tuition is only one reason why more students across the U.S. are entering two-year community colleges first.

(2) Many students say that they enjoy the smaller classes at community colleges. Students also say that teachers are there to teach, not to do research. In many large four-year colleges, freshman courses are taught by graduate assistants, not professors. In community colleges, the classes are taught by the professors. Some students choose a two-year college for this academic quality.

(3) Other students claim that community colleges adjust their programs more to students. They offer many evening classes and part-time programs. They work with business and industry to train students for new jobs in the community. For example, technology training (computers, programming, networking, etc.) and health care training are very popular at community colleges.

(4) Most students attending community colleges are 25–40 years old. They often have jobs and families and want to continue their education or upgrade their job skills. Some community colleges are now offering "e-learn" programs, so students take courses online to earn a degree.

(5) There are many reasons why students are choosing community colleges: low tuition, academic quality, and the availability and flexibility of programs. Enrollment in community colleges is on the rise for all these reasons. Community colleges now enroll about 44 percent of the more than 14 million students attending U.S. colleges and universities. In 1980, they enrolled only 37.4 percent.

As one student said, "Why should I pay all of that money to move away from home, live in a crowded dormitory, and attend large classes taught by graduate assistants? I can live at home, attend a small community college with small classes, work with teachers who care about teaching, and save a bundle of money in the bargain."

NOTE: Information in Reading 4 is adapted from Rajkomar Bimal, "Dual Admission May Improve UC Diversity," *University Wire* (10 June 2000).

Vocabulary from Reading 4

Find these words in Reading 4. Examine the use of each word and guess its meaning. If you are not sure, ask a classmate or check your dictionary.

Nouns	Verbs	Adjectives
availability	adjust	academic
dormitory	enroll	crowded
enrollment	enter	lower
flexibility	increase	on-line
freshman	offer	popular
graduate assistant	transfer	smaller
industry		
networking		**Idioms**
professor		bundle of money
programming		in the bargain
quality		
research		
technology		
tuition		

Vocabulary Work

Part 1

Write these words in the proper categories.

freshman   graduate
computer programming   professor
computer networking   research assistant

People at College   **Courses of Study**

_____   _____

_____   _____

_____   _____

_____   _____

Part 2

Answer these questions from the vocabulary list on page 50. Work in teams of two or three. (NOTE: The questions ask for words from the list.)

1. Which word means *the money students pay to go to classes in school*?

2. Where do some students live at college?

3. What do you call a first-year student at college?

4. What do you call a student who has already finished college or university?

5. "There are too many people in this room." What word describes the room?

6. You want to learn how to connect computers together to share information. What type of course might you take?

7. You want to learn how to make a computer do some work or solve problems. What type of course might you take?

8. What word means *to move from one place to another?*

9. What kind of courses are English, history, math, and science?

Make up other questions about the words on the list to ask your partner(s).

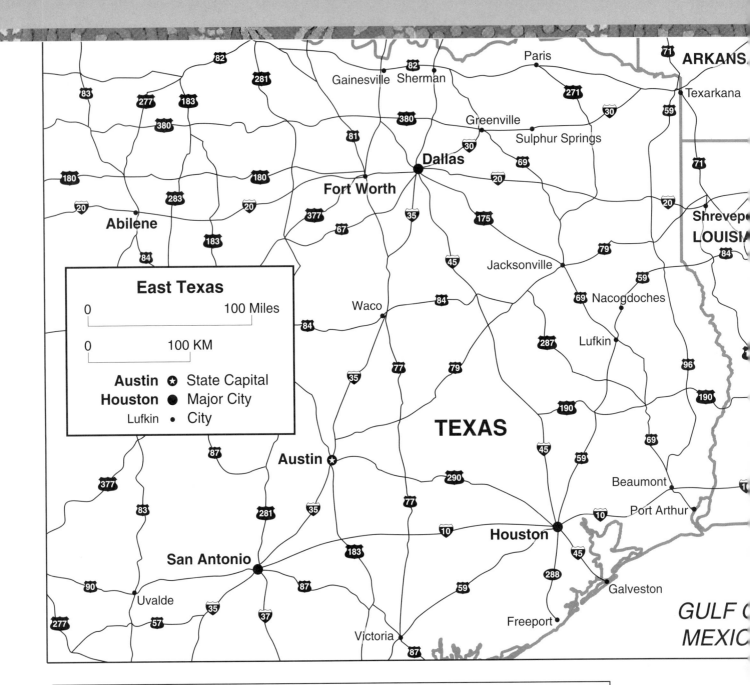

East Texas

0   100 Miles

0   100 KM

Austin ✪ State Capital
Houston ● Major City
Lufkin • City

Map Work

1. Find Houston. Where is Houston in relationship to Austin, the capital of Texas? Where is it in relationship to Dallas?

2. What states border Texas to the east?

3. If students at Texas Southern University or Houston Community College want to drive to the beach, how do they get there? Trace the route.

4. If they want to drive to San Antonio, how do they get there? Tell someone what route to take.

5. Ask your classmates questions about the map.

Taking Notes

Please complete the outline below with information from Reading 4.

**Analysis of Reasons for Rising Enrollments at
U.S. Community Colleges**

I. Cost

    A. lower tuition—e.g., $1,296 (Houston Community College) vs. $2,064 (Texas Southern University)

    B. cheaper to live at home

II. Academic quality

    A. more personal attention from teachers

    B.

    C.

III. Schedules and programs to meet students' needs

    A.

    B.

Exercise A: Punctuating

Use a comma (,) to help a reader separate the parts of a sentence.

> • a city from a state: Los Angeles, California
>
> • a series of three of more items: English, math, and science
>
> • two sentences that are joined with *and, but,* or *or:* Some classes are small, but some classes are very large.
>
> • a quotation: He said, "I'd prefer to go to a community college."

As you copy the sentences below onto a separate page, add commas where needed.

1. Do you want to enroll now for the fall semester or do you want to wait until the spring semester?

2. Texas Southern University is in Houston Texas.

3. The tuition at Texas Southern University is $990 a year but the tuition at Houston Community College is only $640 a year.

4. A technology student should take courses in networking programming and web page design.

5. Students can live at home or they can stay in a dormitory.

6. One student asked "Why should I pay all of that money?"

7. Some reasons for choosing a community college are lower costs smaller classes and more individual attention.

8. The number of students enrolling at community colleges continued to increase in 1988 1990 and 1992.

9. Piedmont Community College in Charlottesville Virginia offers many courses at a reasonable price.

10. "I like the flexibility and part-time programs at this college" said a freshman student.

Exercise B: Comparing and Contrasting

Combine each pair of sentences below into one sentence. Use the word in parentheses and one of the following structures:

- for short adjectives (1–2 syllables):
  adjective + *er than*

OR

- for long adjectives (2+ syllables) and nouns:
  more + adjective/noun *than*

Examples:

In 1990, community colleges enrolled about 6 million students. In 1980, they enrolled about 5 million. (students)
In 1990, community colleges enrolled more students than in 1980.

The professors at the community colleges seemed friendly. The professors at the university did not seem friendly. (friendly)
The professors at the community college seemed friendlier than the professors at the university.

1. At some community colleges, classes are as small as 20–25. At some universities, lecture classes may be as large as 200–250. (small)

   _____

   _____

2. At some community colleges, teachers of freshman courses have a lot of experience. At some universities, teachers of freshman courses are themselves graduate students. (experience)

   _____

   _____

3. Community colleges offer many training programs. Universities offer very few training programs. (training programs)

   _____

   _____

4. Technology and health care training are popular courses for students at community colleges. They are not so popular at universities. (popular)

   _____

   _____

5. Southern Texas University charges $2,064 a year in tuition. Houston Community College charges $1,296 a year. (expensive)

    _____

    _____

6. Community colleges add interesting courses every year. Universities don't add many new courses. (interesting)

    _____

    _____

7. Living at home is comfortable. Living in a dormitory is not always very comfortable. (comfortable)

    _____

    _____

8. The university has a very large library. The community college library is not as large. (large)

    _____

    _____

Exercise C: Paraphrasing

The sentences A–F generally paraphrase sentences 1–6 below. Compare them and then match them.

A. Teachers at community colleges seem to have more time for students.

B. Teachers at community colleges seem to care more about teaching than about research.

C. Community colleges have programs and schedules to fit students' needs.

D. Community college enrollments are increasing faster than those of four-year colleges and universities.

E. Some community colleges and universities are working together so students can finish their degrees at the universities.

F. Students say that cost, better and smaller classes, and job-related programs are reasons to choose community colleges.

_____ 1. Community colleges usually have evening classes and part-time programs for students who work.

_____ 2. Many students can transfer from community colleges to universities to continue their education.

_____ 3. Most teachers at community colleges are there to teach, not to do research.

_____ 4. Low tuition, academic quality, and special training programs are reasons why some students are going to community colleges.

_____ 5. Enrollments at the 1,517 two-year colleges were up about 6 percent in 1990, but they were only up about 3 percent in four-year colleges and universities.

_____ 6. Students at community colleges say that they get more personal attention from their teachers.

Notes and Questions on Reading 4

Part A: Paragraphs

Reading 4 describes a trend, a general change of direction. The writer analyzes (thinks about and explains) why people are doing one thing and not another thing. In Reading 4, more people are choosing community colleges than before. The writer explains why people prefer X to Y.

Look at Reading 4 as introduction, body, and conclusion. See how the writer has organized the composition. The following questions will help you understand the organization:

1. In which paragraph do you first begin to see the writer's plan? Does the writer tell you directly what will follow? Do you think the writer should say, "There are three reasons why enrollments at U.S. community colleges are rising"?

2. Does Reading 4 have an introduction? Where does the body begin? Where is the rest of the body?

3. Where does the conclusion begin? How does the writer conclude?

Part B: Order

Writers analyze in different ways. The writer of Reading 4 analyzes a trend by explaining the reasons for it. The writer explains each reason with supporting details.

In Reading 4, what is the trend? What are the reasons for it? Let these questions lead you to the answers:

1. Where do you learn the first reason?

2. Where do you read the second reason? Where does the writer actually "name" the second reason—give it a label?

3. Where do you read the third reason? Where does the writer give it a label?

4. Where does the writer summarize all of the reasons?

This way of dividing a topic—in this reading, a trend—into parts is called *partition*. There is only one topic, but there are several parts to it.

Preliminary Writing

You and your teacher can decide which of the following activities to do. They will help you prepare for your own composition. Write in your journal or in your notebook.

1. You are trying to decide where to go to college—a community college near your home or a university far away. Make a list of the reasons for going to each. List both good points and bad points. Then state your decision and the reasons for it. (You do not have to agree with the writer of Reading 4.)

2. You are planning to be a college professor. Decide if you want to teach in a community college or not. Write about your reasons.

3. You are a parent. Your only child wants to go far away to study at an expensive university. Write down the reasons for wanting your child to stay at home and go to the community college nearby.

4. Think of an important decision you made some time ago. What reasons did you have then? Do you think your reasons were good? Did you make the right decision?

5. Think of a decision (large or small) that a friend is trying to make. Explain what she or he is trying to decide. Then, make two lists: reasons *for* and reasons *against*. Which decision is better? Write your friend and give him or her advice.

6. Make a list of the decisions that most of the people you know have to make in life. Write each decision using *either...or.* For example, "either go to college or work full time."

Composition 4 (Analysis by Contrast)

Instructions for Composition 4

Please follow the instructions below. Work in pairs whenever possible, especially with numbers 2–5 and 8–9.

1. Think of a current trend. For example: fewer and fewer teenagers are using drugs, the rate of crime is down, or more and more people are traveling by air. You will need to analyze the trend. What are the reasons for it? What is causing the trend? (See more suggested topics on the following page.)

2. Make a list of reasons why this trend is happening. If you can't think of at least three reasons, try another subject.

3. Note examples, statistics, personal experience, etc. to help explain and support the reasons.

4. Interview a classmate to find out why she or he thinks this trend is happening. Ask for your classmate's personal knowledge or experience with your topic. (Later, find a way to include some of your classmate's opinions in your composition.)

5. Go over your notes. Add new ideas that come to you. Circle those that you want to build into your composition.

6. Write out a draft of your composition. Use Reading 4 as a model. As in Reading 4, you can begin with details and then explain the reasons and the trend. Go on from there, explaining and supporting each of your additional reasons. After you finish writing, read over your draft. See if it says what you want it to say. Make changes where necessary.

7. Check your draft against these questions:
    *   Do you clearly explain why something is happening?
    *   Do you explain with at least three reasons?
    *   Do you give details or support for each reason?
    *   Are these reasons important?
    *   Do you summarize the reasons in your conclusion?

8. Continue to make changes as you reread your composition. Pass it to a classmate to see if your ideas are clear. Think about your reader's (classmate's) questions and comments. Make changes where necessary.

9. When you think you have done all you can do, proofread your composition. Check the following: title, margins, indented paragraphs, capital letters, punctuation, spelling, and grammar. Make any necessary changes as you proofread. Then, wait for your teacher's instructions.

Suggested Topics for Composition 4

Analyze the following trends:

1. The number of homeless people is increasing.

2. More and more marriages are ending in divorce.

3. Fewer and fewer teenagers are using drugs.

4. Fewer people in the U.S. are smoking these days.

5. More and more people are traveling by air.

6. The rate of crime in the city is decreasing.

7. The world's supply of air and water is becoming more and more polluted.

8. More of the world's forests are being cut down.

9. More and more women are working outside the home.

10. More and more people own a home computer.

 # Connecting

Search the Internet for information about the trend you chose. You may want to find the name of a company, government agency, or organization that works with this trend. Can you find information to explain and support the reasons for the trend? Share the information you find with a partner. Check if you can use the information in your composition.

Generalizing

A traditional herbalist grinds and mixes medicinal herbs in her shop.

Plants have provided the world with powerful medicines.
A few examples are shown below.

Rauvolfia:
to combat high
blood pressure

Rosy Periwinkle:
to treat childhood
leukemia

Cinchona:
to treat malaria

Chondrondendron:
to relax muscles
during surgery

Foxglove:
to treat heart problems

Look at the illustrations.

- What do these plants have in common?
- What is the relationship between plants and medical treatment?
- What do you think you will read about?

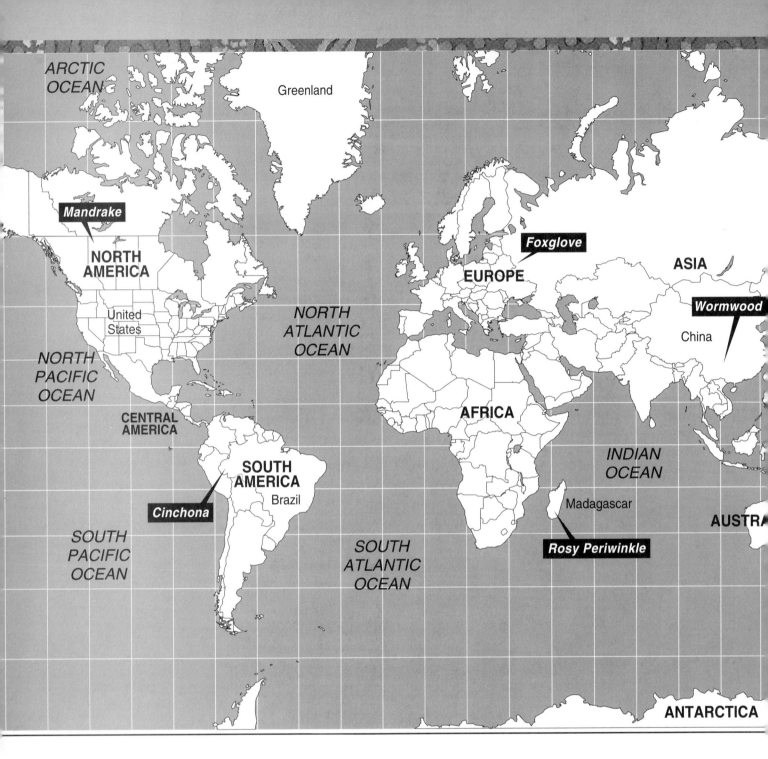

ARCTIC OCEAN

Greenland

Mandrake

NORTH AMERICA

United States

NORTH PACIFIC OCEAN

NORTH ATLANTIC OCEAN

CENTRAL AMERICA

Foxglove

EUROPE

ASIA

Wormwood

China

AFRICA

INDIAN OCEAN

Madagascar

AUSTRA

SOUTH AMERICA

Brazil

Cinchona

SOUTH PACIFIC OCEAN

SOUTH ATLANTIC OCEAN

Rosy Periwinkle

ANTARCTICA

Map Work

1. Where is Brazil? On which continent is it located?

2. Where is Madagascar?

3. Where is China? On which continent is it found?

4. Where does the foxglove plant grow?

5. Ask your classmates questions about the map.

Reading 5

The Medicinal Value of Plants

(1) Today we go to the pharmacy or drugstore to buy medicine when we are sick. But where did people get medicine before there were pharmacies and drugstores? What did people use to fight diseases? For hundreds and thousands of years, people have used plants as sources for medicines. They used different parts of the plants—the roots, the leaves, the flowers, and the bark. Today, doctors are beginning to rediscover the value and importance of some plants. Over 120 different kinds of medicine come from a hundred different species of plants. Plants are the source for nearly a quarter of all prescription drugs. Let's look at some examples.

(2) Aspirin is a common medicine. When we take an aspirin, we are taking a chemical from the bark of the *willow tree*. For hundreds of years, people have used *foxglove* to make the heart slow down. Recently, scientists have developed another drug from the same plant. This new drug helps prevent heart problems. In tropical areas, malaria has been a problem. Scientists have learned that the bark of a South American tree, the *cinchona,* can be used to make quinine. Quinine is a drug that helps prevent malaria..

(3) For a long time, the Chinese have known that *wormwood* can also fight malaria. Scientists have been working with the wormwood plant to develop new drugs against malaria. Another example of a plant with medicinal value is the *mandrake.* For hundreds of years, Native Americans have used the root of the mandrake to treat sick people. Recently, doctors have "discovered" medicine from the mandrake. They have been using it as a treatment for lung cancer.

(4) People on the island of Madagascar have traditionally used the leaves of the *rosy periwinkle* for various health problems. Today, doctors use a medicine from the rosy periwinkle to treat children with leukemia, a kind of blood cancer. This "new" medicine has increased the rate of survival from leukemia.

(5) Most people are familiar with garlic as an ingredient in different foods. In Germany, scientists completed a four-year study on garlic. They found that garlic helps prevent the build-up of plaque, a material in the blood system. Too much plaque can make it difficult for the blood to pass through the arteries. The people who took the garlic powder had fewer heart-related problems than those who didn't take the powder. This very common plant continues to be studied.

(6)   Many of these studies were before 1960 when animals were used in laboratory experiments over long periods of time. Now, new technology is making it possible for scientists to test drugs more quickly and without hurting animals. So far, scientists have been focusing on plants from the rain forests of Brazil and Southeast Asia. There are about 250,000 species of flowering plants in the world, and most of these plants are in the rain forests! Scientists have studied little more than one percent of plants for their medicinal value. Maybe cures for AIDS and cancer exist somewhere in the other 99 percent.

NOTE: Information in Reading 5 is adapted from: "Biodiversity's Contribution to Medicine," World Resource Institute; Mitzi Perdue, "A Treasure Trove for Future Generations," *The Environment and You*; and "DNA and the New Generation of Drugs."

Vocabulary from Reading 5

Find these words in Reading 5. Examine the use of each word and guess its meaning. If you are not sure, ask a classmate or check your dictionary.

Nouns	Verbs	Adjectives
artery	develop	common
aspirin	fight	tropical
bark	focus	
blood	prevent	
chemical	rediscover	
cure	treat	
disease		
heart		
leukemia		
lung cancer		
malaria		
pharmacy		
plaque		
prescription drug		
quinine		
root		
source		
species		
survival		
treatment		
value		

Vocabulary Work

Part 1

Write these words in the proper categories.

aspirin	bark	artery	disease
heart	leukemia	lung cancer	malaria
prescription drug	quinine	root	

Health Problems	Parts of a Plant	Parts of the Body	Medicines
_____	_____	_____	_____
_____	_____	_____	_____
_____	_____	_____	_____
_____	_____	_____	_____

Part 2

Answer these questions using the vocabulary list on page 66. Work in pairs. (NOTE: The questions ask for words from the list.)

1. What part of a plant grows under the ground?

2. What is the outer covering of a tree called?

3. Where can you buy medicine?

4. Which word means to "find again"?

5. What is the opposite of "rare"?

6. What is the name of a kind of blood cancer?

7. Which word describes an area where the weather is very hot and wet all year?

8. Which word means to make something new or make something happen?

9. Which word means to keep something from happening?

10. What is the place (or thing) where something comes from?

Make up other questions about the words on the list to ask your partner.

Taking Notes

Please complete the notes below with information from Reading 5.

Generalization: *Plants provide the world with many medicines.*

Supporting examples:

PLANT	USES
1. willow tree	makes aspirin
2.	
3. foxglove	makes heart slow down / prevents heart problems
4.	
5.	
6.	

Exercise A: Using the Present Perfect Tense

Please write the present perfect form of the verbs in parentheses. Use the present perfect tense for actions that started in the past and continue to the present time.

present perfect = *have/has* + past participle

Example: In parts of South America and Asia, malaria *has been* (be) a health problem.

1. For ten years, Dr. Jones _____ (work) in the Brazilian rain forest.

2. She _____ (examine) many new plants there.

3. Scientists _____ (learn) many things about medicinal plants from other cultures.

4. Since 1970, herbal medicines _____ (become) more popular in the United States.

5. Many immigrants _____ (bring) new ideas for medical treatment from their native cultures.

6. For hundreds of years, Native Americans _____ (use) willow bark to treat headaches.

7. Recently, scientists _____ (develop) new drugs from plants.

8. These new drugs _____ (help) many sick people.

9. So far, scientists _____ not _____ (discover) a cure for cancer.

Exercise B: Using the Present Perfect and Simple Present Tenses

Write the simple present or the present perfect to complete the sentences below. Use the simple present tense for repeated or habitual actions in the present and for true facts. Use the present perfect tense for actions that started in the past and continue to the present time.

Examples: Modern doctors *need* (need) to learn more.

The Chinese *have known* (know) about medicinal plants for centuries.

1. We often _____ (take) aspirin for a headache.

2. For hundreds of years, people _____ (use) the foxglove plant to slow down the heart.

3. Recently, scientists _____ (develop) a drug from foxglove to prevent heart problems.

4. For a thousand years, the Chinese people _____ (know) how to use wormwood to fight malaria.

5. For hundreds of years, Native Americans _____ (treat) sick people with the mandrake plant.

6. Today, scientists _____ (use) medicines from the mandrake plant to treat lung cancer.

7. For a long time, people on the island of Madagascar _____ (make) medicines from the rosy periwinkle plant.

8. Over the past few years, a new medicine _____ (increase) the rate of survival from leukemia.

9. Now scientists _____ (want) to study the plants in the rain forest.

10. Until now, scientists _____ (study) only one percent of these 250,000 plants for their medicinal value.

Exercise C: Writing Numbers

Complete each sentence below with the word in parentheses. Tell about the general quantity. Use the plural number word + *of.*

> *Examples:* The rain forest has _thousands of_ species of flowering plants. (thousand)
>
> The rain forest really has _hundreds of thousands of_ kinds of flowering plants. (hundred thousand)

1. The state of Michigan produces _____ bushels of apples each year. (thousand)

2. The Middle East produces _____ barrels of crude oil each year. (million)

3. The United States government gives _____ dollars to doctors and scientists for research each year. (million)

4. The People's Republic of China occupies _____ square miles of land. (million)

5. _____ people in the United States die each year from guns. (thousand)

6. In the United States, you can drive _____ miles in a day because the highway system is so good. (hundred)

7. The state of Minnesota produces _____ bushels of corn and grain each year. (hundred thousand)

8. Doctors save _____ children each year with a drug from the rosy periwinkle. (thousand)

9. _____ people around the world don't have enough food to eat. (hundred thousand)

10. In the state of California, there are _____ miles of highway. (ten thousand)

Exercise D: Drawing Conclusions

A generalization is a general statement. Match the following generalizations with the specific examples below. Write out each generalization on the appropriate line. Then, discuss with your teacher why each generalization is an appropriate final statement.

> A. So, it is important to save the rain forest.
>
> B. These examples show that people have used plants as medicine for a long time.
>
> C. In conclusion, plants are used to make important medicines for people around the world.
>
> D. This shows that foxglove is a very valuable plant.
>
> E. People in all different parts of the world have known how to use plants for medicines.

1. For thousands of years, the Chinese have used the wormwood plant to fight malaria, and the people of Madagascar have used the rosy periwinkle for treating diseases.

   (B) These examples show that people have used plants as medicine for a long time.

2. Medicine from the European plant foxglove can be used to slow down the heart. Doctors have also developed another medicine from the same plant to prevent heart problems.

   _____

   _____

3. The native people of North and South America and of Asia have known for hundreds of years that plants can be used as medicines. People of Africa have also treated diseases with medicine from plants.

_____

_____

4. In the Amazon, many plant species are in danger. Those plants might give us medicine to cure cancer.

_____

_____

5. Quinine, a medicine used to prevent malaria, comes from the bark of a tree. A drug from the root of the mandrake is used to treat lung cancer. A chemical from the rosy periwinkle can be used to treat leukemia.

_____

_____

Notes and Questions on Reading 5

Part A: Paragraphs

Reading 5 is about this generalization: *Plants are important for medicines around the world*. The reading supports or proves the generalization with many examples. The reader probably agrees with this general statement because the examples are clear and strong.

Look at the paragraphs in Reading 5. Think about how the paragraphs are divided. The following questions may help:

1. Where does the writer introduce the main generalization?

2. Where does the writer begin to give specific examples to support or prove the general statement?

3. How many paragraphs have specific examples? What do the examples teach you about native and "modern" uses of plants?

4. How does the writer conclude? What effect does the conclusion have on you? How does it support the writer's general statement?

Part B: Order

Check to make sure that you understood the order of information in Reading 5 by answering the following questions:

1. Which is the most important sentence in the whole essay? Why is it the most important? (Another word you will hear for this kind of sentence is "thesis," the writer's main point.)

2. Which paragraph is more specific: paragraph 1 or paragraph 2?

3. How many different examples does the writer give to support the thesis or main point?

4. How is the information in the conclusion different from the information in the second and third paragraphs? Why do you think the writer put it last?

Reading 5 starts with a generalization. Then it shows the reader some specific examples. Of course, the writer uses the examples to support or prove the generalization.

Preliminary Writing

You and your teacher can decide which of the following activities to do. Write in your journal or in your notebook.

1. Take any of the following generalizations. Think of three or four examples to "prove" the point. Then, write a paragraph, beginning with the generalization.

    • The cost of health care is rising.
    • Tuition for schools is going up.
    • The quality of the products we buy is going down.
    • A good man (or woman) is hard to find.
    • An education is necessary for a good job.

2. Imagine that you are a parent. (Maybe you are, so you don't need to use your imagination!) Think of one very important lesson that you want to teach your children. Write it down as a generalization. Write three or four examples that will get your children's attention.

3. Make a list of generalizations that you can personally make from daily life. Before you write the generalizations, make sure you have three or four particular examples to support each one. You can make these generalizations from your own experiences, from things a friend told you, etc.

4. Go back to Exercise D on page 71. Rewrite each item, but begin each one with the generalization. Put the examples into your own words. Add other examples if you can. Make other changes where necessary.

Composition 5 (Generalizations and Examples)

Instructions for Composition 5

Please follow the instructions below. Work in pairs whenever possible, especially with numbers 2–4 and 6–7.

1. Think of a conclusion that you have drawn from personal experience or from other people. It may be about you or your family, or it may be about society in general. Choose something you really think is important. (Check the suggestions on the following page, if you need ideas.) Imagine you are writing for people who need to learn about your topic.

2. State your conclusion as a generalization. Make a list of examples to support it. Be sure to have strong examples that will "prove" your point. Do you have examples that you can develop with exact details?

3. From your list, choose three or four of the best examples. Circle the ones you want to include in your composition.

4. To help you organize your ideas, look back at the notes on page 68. Make notes like these.

5. When your plan is complete, write a draft of your composition. Read it over and see what changes you want to make. Ask a classmate to read it and tell what is clear and what is not clear.

6. Check your draft against these questions:

   • Do you start with a general statement? Is it a generalization that your reader will really care about?

   • Do you have other general comments to make before you begin your examples?

   • Do you show enough good examples to your reader?

   • Is your conclusion interesting? Does it do more than repeat your main idea?

7. Continue to make changes as you read and reread your writing. Then, proofread your essay. Check the following: title, margins, paragraph divisions, indentation, capital letters, punctuation, and spelling.

8. If appropriate, add charts, diagrams, or pictures to support your writing.

Suggested Topics for Composition 5

Draw a generalization from the following:

1. Your opinion about the quality of child care in your area

2. Your opinion on the cost of medical insurance

3. Your experience in getting medical insurance

4. Your opinion on a national health program

5. Your opinion on an alternative medical treatment, such as acupuncture, massage, acupressure, etc.

6. Your opinion on the difficulties of raising children

7. Your positive experience as a student in a particular educational system

8. Same as 7 (above), but your negative experience

9. Your opinion on the value of exercise and good nutrition

10. Your experience with the dangers of smoking

11. Your experience with the difficulties immigrants have keeping their own culture alive

12. Your opinion on a social issue important to you, with examples from personal experience or from the newspaper

13. Your opinion on the importance of parents' involvement in their children's education

14. Your opinion on an economic issue important to you, with examples from newspapers, magazines, and/or personal experience

15. Your experience with discrimination against women, people from your culture, or people who speak English with an accent

16. Your experience in handling a difficult situation

 # Connecting

Search the Internet for information on herbal medicines or other choices for health care. What types of problems do they treat? How much do they cost? What other information can you find about these alternatives to traditional medical treatments? Share the information you find with a partner.

Unit 6 Arguing a Point

The Jivaro, an Indian people of Peru, hunt animals with arrows rubbed in a paralyzing poison.

Composition Focus: Argumentation

Organizational Focus: Induction

Grammatical Focus: Tenses in Contrast
Modals

Examining plants on an expedition on the Amazon River

Look at the photos and the map.

● Who are these people?

● How do they use plants?

● What do you think you will read about?

Reading 6

The Rain Forest: What Is It Worth?

(1) It contains more than 4,000 types of birds and more than 1,000,000 types of insects. In one square mile, there may be more than 100 different types of plants. Some call it the world's last wilderness area. People are becoming concerned. They want to protect this last wilderness area, the rain forest, and its plant and animal life. In Costa Rica, students have raised money to buy land in the rain forest to protect it. Some businesses prefer to buy products from the rain forest to encourage leaving the forest as it is. Others, such as a major ice cream maker, have been giving a percentage of their profits for rain forest protection. Scientists have realized that native peoples of the rain forest have great knowledge of the medical value of plants there.

(2) In the rain forest of the Amazon, 50 to 150 plant species are being destroyed every day. Some people want to use the land, so they cut down some of the rain forest. They want the trees for wood to build houses. They want the land to grow grass for cattle. They want to build roads to areas for mining gold and other minerals. As a result, the forest and its plants are disappearing. Because native people live in and need the forest for survival, they too are disappearing. In Brazil alone, more than 90 tribes have disappeared since 1900. Thousands of years of knowledge have disappeared with these people. Other tribes have lost or forgotten their old ways. The young people do not want to learn from the old people.

(3) Some scientists and anthropologists are pointing out the importance of the plants and knowledge of the tribes. They say that it is time to put an economic value on the rain forest. It will show the peoples of the rain forests that the world values them, their knowledge of the plants, and the plants themselves. This might be the only way to save these people, the plants, and the forests.

(4) Some companies and organizations are also beginning to change. They are signing agreements with the native people. For example, native people collect plants in the rain forest for the National Cancer Institute. The institute is developing drugs from these plants. It now agrees to share a percentage of the money it receives from these drugs with the native people. A drug

company in California also has promised to share profits with the native collectors of drugs developed from rain forest plants. Some other groups are helping tribes sell rain forest products such as herbs and oils. These efforts are still unusual, but they are a start.

(5)   What is the alternative? The alternative is that the plants will disappear, and the native people will disappear with them. The knowledge that might save you or me from cancer, heart disease, or AIDS might also disappear. Modern medicine still needs the healing arts of native people.

(6)   The people who live in the rain forest countries are beginning to see that it is profitable and important to save these areas. The Jivaro, a tribe in the rain forest of northern Peru, recently told some scientists, "You are like babies in the rain forest, but we will teach you." The Jivaro tribe knows the secrets and value of the plants and rain forest. Let's hope that we and the scientists are smart enough to learn from them.

NOTE: Information in Reading 6 is adapted from Joseph Wallace, "Rainforest Rx," and Noreen Parks, "Who Owns the Rosy Periwinkle?" by *Sierra*, Vol. 76/No. 4 (July/August, 1991): 36–41.

The Rain Forest

Vocabulary from Reading 6

Find these words in Reading 6. Examine the use of each word and guess its meaning. If you are not sure, ask a classmate or check your dictionary.

Nouns	Verbs	Adjectives
agreement	destroy	economic
alternative	disappear	profitable
anthropologist	forget	unusual
cattle	lose	
effort	mine	
gold	promise	
healing arts	share	
herb	value	
mineral		
native people		
nature		
oil		
organization		
percentage		
profit		
tribe		

Vocabulary Work

Part 1

Match the words below with their meanings.

_____ 1. forget

_____ 2. destroy

_____ 3. disappear

_____ 4. lose

_____ 5. agreement

_____ 6. mine

_____ 7. profit

_____ 8. share

_____ 9. unusual

_____ 10. profitable

a. not to be able to find or keep something

b. not common

c. to dig in the earth to get something such as gold

d. not to remember

e. making money; rewarding

f. to tear down; to ruin

g. to stop being

h. an understanding or arrangement between groups

i. to divide between partners

j. money made in business

Part 2

Answer these questions using the vocabulary list on page 80. Work in pairs.

1. How do we refer to all living things?

2. What do we call a person who studies people's cultures?

3. What is another word for another possibility?

4. You *give your word*. What do you do?

5. What do we call a group of people who work together for a specific purpose?

6. You ask, "How much money is something worth?" What do you want to know?

7. Thousands of years ago, there were no modern medicines. What did people use when someone was sick or hurt?

8. What are things found in nature, such as gold or iron?

9. What is one type of animal that people keep for meat or dairy products?

10. What do we call a group of people usually of the same families or culture?

Make up other questions about the words on the list to ask your partner.

South America

✪	National Capital
•	City
—	River
—	Continent Boundary
—	State Boundary
BOLIVIA	Country Name

0   500 Miles

0   500 KM

Map Work

1. Trace the Amazon River. Does it flow to the east or to the west? What countries does it flow through? Where does it end?

2. Find Rio de Janeiro. Where is it located?

3. What South American countries border the Pacific Ocean? What bodies of water surround South America?

4. Where is Venezuela? Where is Peru, the home of the Jivaro?

5. Ask your classmates questions about the map.

Taking Notes

Please complete the outline below with information from Reading 6.

Argument: Writer Wants to Save the Rain Forest

I. Reasons for saving the rain forest

    A. to preserve plants, many with medicinal value

    B.

    C. perhaps to save our lives, with treatment from medicinal plants

II. Present and future reasons for saving the rain forest

    A. plants: 50–150 species destroyed every day

    B.

    C.

III. Ways to save the rain forest

    A. share money earned from using rain forest plants

    B.

    C.

Exercise A: Using Modals

Use *might, must, can, could,* or *will* to answer the questions below.
Answer in full sentences according to the information in Reading 6.
Check back to the reading if you are not sure of an answer.

1. What is going to happen if the rain forest is not saved?

2. What is the possible effect for you and me of saving the rain forest?

3. What is the writer's main argument in this essay? What result does the
   writer strongly suggest?

4. How does the writer strongly argue that this will happen?

5. What is your advice to modern scientists and doctors?

Exercise B: Sorting Out Reasons

Reading 6 gives reasons in favor of saving the rain forest. Most arguments
have two sides—for and against. Look at the arguments below about the
rain forest. Notice how the points are divided into positive *(for)* or
negative *(against)* groups.

Example: **Argument:** Should we save the rain forest?

SAVE THE RAIN FOREST?	
FOR (yes!):	**AGAINST (no!):**
To protect plants for medicine	Trees are needed for wood for houses and building the economy
To protect the knowledge of native people	Land is needed for grass, for cattle, for food for people from cattle
To save our lives with treatments from medicinal plants	Land is needed to develop mining, the economy needs profits from mining

Now, look at the three arguments below. Divide the points into positive *(for)* or negative *(against)* groups.

1. **Argument:** Is it better to live in a city or not?

   Points to consider: dirty air
   noise
   near medical services
   near schools
   high rent
   stores open 24 hours a day
   near theaters and restaurants

LIVE IN THE CITY?	
FOR:	AGAINST:

2. **Argument:** Should a student study in a foreign country?

   Points to consider: learn a new language
   away from family and old friends
   educational opportunities
   new culture
   alone
   expensive
   away from problems at home
   make new friends

STUDY IN A NEW COUNTRY?	
FOR:	AGAINST:

3. **Argument:** Is it better to take public transportation or to drive yourself?

Points to consider: read on the way
wait for bus/train
save money on gasoline
worry about safety at night
relax on the way
no worry about parking
privacy

TAKE PUBLIC TRANSPORTATION?	
FOR:	AGAINST:

Exercise C: Organizing Inductively

Write your own reasons for the conclusions below.

Example: 1. *buy gasoline*
2. *pay for car insurance*
3. *pay for repairs*
4. *pay for regular maintenance*

Therefore, it is expensive to own a car.

A. 1.

2.

3.

4.

In summary, a foreigner has many problems to face in a new country.

B. 1.

   2.

   3.

   4.

   Therefore, people who smoke should quit.

C. 1.

   2.

   3.

   4.

   So, it is not easy to live in a large city.

D. 1.

   2.

   3.

   4.

   The English language is difficult to learn.

E. 1.

   2.

   3.

   4.

   As a result, immigrant families should speak their native languages at home.

Notes and Questions on Reading 6

Part A: Paragraphs

Reading 6 argues a position. The writer has a point of view that she wants everyone to accept. Therefore, she presents only one side of the argument: *we must not let the rain forests disappear.* In this way, the writer tries to show that the alternative to her position is not acceptable.

Arguments have two sides, at least. A writer may include reasons both for and against. It all depends on the writer and the subject.

Look at the paragraphs in Reading 6 to find the writer's logic. These questions may help:

1. Why does the writer use so many specific details in the first paragraph? Why doesn't the writer just come right out and say, "We must save the rain forest!"

2. What information do you learn in the second paragraph? How does this fit into the writer's argument?

3. Where does the writer tell you how the rain forest can be saved?

4. What is new in the fifth paragraph? What is its purpose?

5. How does the writer conclude? What effect does the quotation have?

Part B: Order
Writers usually build their arguments in one of two ways. They may start with specifics that lead to a generalization, or start with a generalization supported by specifics. The two types of organization look something like this:

GENERALIZATION

SPECIFICS

SPECIFICS

GENERALIZATION

1. Does Reading 6 start with specifics or with a general point?

2. Where do you first learn the writer's real position?

Reading 5 was an example of starting with a generalization and supporting it with details *(deductive logic)*. Reading 6 presents the specifics and then shows the generalization *(inductive logic)*.

Preliminary Writing

You and your teacher can decide which of the following activities to do. Write in your journal or in your notebook.

1. Make a list of arguments that you hear all around you. For example, should young people wait until they are older to get married? Is it better to wait a few years before going to college?

2. Make a list of the reasons you have heard for and against going to college.

3. Make a list of the major social or political arguments currently in the newspapers or on TV.

4. Write about a point of disagreement in your family or neighborhood. Explain the reasons that people give for and against this particular point. Try to present reasons for and against.

5. Write about an issue that was very important to you when you were younger. This may be an issue that seems unimportant to you now. Explain your reasons as you remember them. Explain the change in your point of view as you got older.

Composition 6 (Argumentation)

Instructions for Composition 6

Please follow the instructions below. Work in pairs whenever possible, especially with numbers 2–4 and 6.

1. From your preliminary writing or from the suggested topics on the following page, choose one point or issue that you want to write more about. Perhaps it is an issue that others have strong feelings about. Perhaps it is important only to you. Decide on who you want to persuade about this issue. Write down who your readers are.

2. Make a list of all the reasons that you can think of *in support of* your position. Also make a list of reasons *against* or *alternatives to* your position.

3. Note facts, figures, examples, or comments that will convince your readers.

4. From your lists and notes, circle the words and ideas that you want to include. Select carefully.

5. Check your draft against these questions:

   • Does your introduction make your reader care about your subject?

   • Do you include enough details to convince your reader?

   • Do you make your argument clear? Do you state *how* readers can meet your goal(s)? Do you explain *why* your readers should agree with you?

   • Do you conclude by adding something of interest?

6. Continue to make changes as you read and reread your writing. Ask a classmate to read it and tell you if something is unclear. When it says what you want it to say, then proofread your essay.

   • Check the following: title, margins, indentation, well-developed paragraphs, capital letters, punctuation, and spelling.

Make any necessary changes. Then, follow your teacher's instructions.

Suggested Topics for Composition 6

Argue one of the following:

1. Fathers should spend more time with their children.

2. Community colleges offer students a better bargain than four-year colleges.

3. Parents and schools should encourage children to keep and develop their home language.

4. Divorce is sometimes a solution to problems between husbands and wives.

5. Smokers should be allowed to smoke on the job and in restaurants.

6. Parents of young children should be allowed to adjust their work schedules.

7. The price of gasoline needs to rise so more people will take public transportation to work.

8. Parents need to be active in their children's schools and education.

9. Women, not government, have the right to make their own decisions about abortion.

10. All people should have medical insurance and medical care.

11. People should express their feelings by writing and talking about them.

12. Marijuana should (not) be legalized.

13. Military service should (not) be voluntary.

14. Old people should be cared for by their families.

15. Parents should have unpaid time off from work to stay at home with their young children.

 # Connecting

Search the Internet for information on saving the rain forests. What countries have tropical rain forests? Do they have national parks or areas that preserve parts of their rain forests? What types of products are available from the rain forest? What international organizations help save the rain forests? Are there any organizations that suggest ways to use the rain forest areas without destroying the trees, plants, and native groups? Share the information you find with a partner or with your class.

Describing Personal Characteristics

Robert Allen, 41, who was born in rural poverty and taught himself to read, will soon receive his doctorate in English literature from Vanderbilt University.

Vanderbilt University in Nashville, Tennessee

- **Composition Focus:** Biography
- **Organizational Focus:** Chronological Order
- **Grammatical Focus:** Simple Past Tense
  Past Perfect Tense

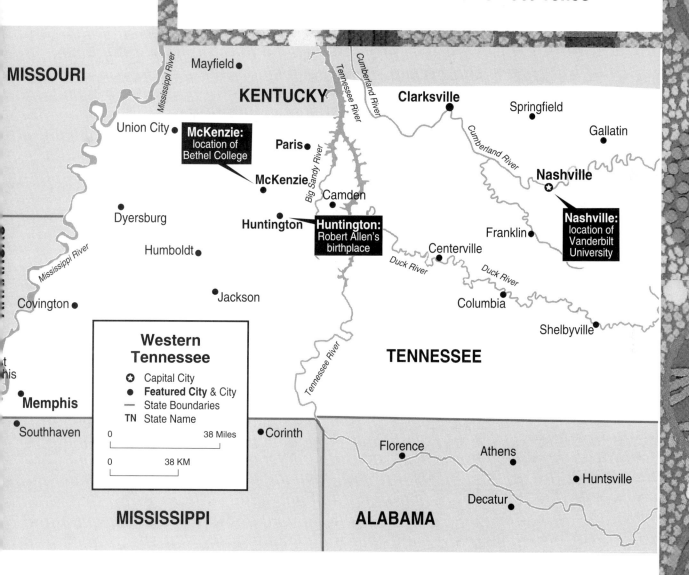

MISSOURI

KENTUCKY

Mayfield

Tennessee River

Cumberland River

Clarksville

Springfield

Gallatin

Union City

McKenzie: location of Bethel College

Paris

Nashville: location of Vanderbilt University

McKenzie

Big Sandy River

Camden

Nashville

Dyersburg

Huntington

Huntington: Robert Allen's birthplace

Franklin

Mississippi River

Humboldt

Centerville

Duck River

Duck River

Jackson

Covington

Columbia

Shelbyville

Western Tennessee

✪ Capital City
● **Featured City** & City
— State Boundaries
TN State Name

0   38 Miles

0   38 KM

TENNESSEE

Memphis

Southhaven

Corinth

Florence

Athens

Huntsville

Tennessee River

Decatur

MISSISSIPPI

ALABAMA

Look at the photos and the map.

- What kind of a person do you think this man is?
- What can you guess about his life?
- What seems unusual about him?
- What does the map tell you?
- How is the map related to the photos?

Reading 7

Love of Learning

(1) Robert Allen was 31 years old when he walked into a classroom for the very first time. Then, eleven years later, he was ready to receive his doctorate in literature. Robert Allen is a lesson in determination for all people. His life is a remarkable story.

(2) Robert Allen was raised by his grandfather in the mountains of Tennessee. For many years, they lived in a poor, rural community 90 miles west of Nashville. His grandfather did not want him to go to school. Instead, his grandfather taught him carpentry. From a young age, Robert made a living with his hands. Somewhere and somehow, Robert taught himself to read from comic books and a family Bible. He had begun to buy books for a dime apiece at yard sales. He probably bought and read more than 2,000 of them.

(3) Back then, few people in Robert's community knew about his love of reading and learning. In fact, most people thought he was slow or stupid. He always dressed in old, worn-out clothes. He spoke to almost no one, and he lived with just his grandfather, separate from the rest of the community. But one person did know Robert Allen. That was the county librarian, Claudine Halpers. She talked to Robert when he came to the library. She suggested books for him to read. She said that Robert read his way through the library. In other words, he actually read everything there.

(4) Claudine Halpers also suggested to Robert that he needed a formal education. She encouraged him to take the high school equivalency test (GED). A year later, he entered Bethel College, a small, four-year college nearby. Gene McMahan, one of his teachers at Bethel, remembers the day Robert walked into his sociology class. Robert was dressed poorly and he looked odd. Professor McMahan was shocked when Robert began to speak. Robert was a "walking encyclopedia," the professor recalled.

(5) The teachers at Bethel "adopted" Robert. They sent him to the dentist, bought him clothes, and helped him understand the machines and technology around him. Robert had never used an elevator, gotten coffee from a machine in the school cafeteria, or used a pay telephone. Robert graduated from Bethel in three years with a 3.9 (out of 4.0) grade average. He got A's in every class except typing.

(6) The teachers at Bethel urged Robert to continue his education. He received a scholarship and enrolled in the graduate program in literature at Vanderbilt University in Nashville. Nashville was the farthest he had ever been from home. When Robert was ready to graduate with both his master's and his doctorate degrees, he was thinking about his future. The first thing he planned to do, he said, was get a job.

Vocabulary from Reading 7

Find these words in Reading 7. Examine the use of each word and guess its meaning. If you are not sure, ask a classmate or check your dictionary.

Nouns	Verbs	Adjectives
carpentry	adopt	farthest
comic book	graduate	formal
determination	raise	odd
doctorate	recall	remarkable
elevator	urge	rural
encyclopedia		shocked
GED	**Adverbs**	worn-out
high school	actually	
equivalency test	apiece	**Others**
librarian	poorly	except
literature	separate	with his hands
master's		
scholarship		
sociology		
technology		
yard sale		

Vocabulary Work

Answer these questions using the vocabulary list on page 95. Work in pairs.

1. What is another word for *Ph.D.*?

2. What is another way to say *strong will?*

3. What do we call *working with wood?*

4. What is the *GED?*

5. What do we call *a large book or set of books full of information, with the subjects in alphabetical order?*

6. What type of area is the opposite of a city?

7. What is another word for *modern machines we use?*

8. What is another way to say *to take a person into your family?*

9. What is another word to describe someone who is *very special?*

10. What is another way to describe someone who is *very strange?*

Make up other questions about the words on the list to ask your partner.

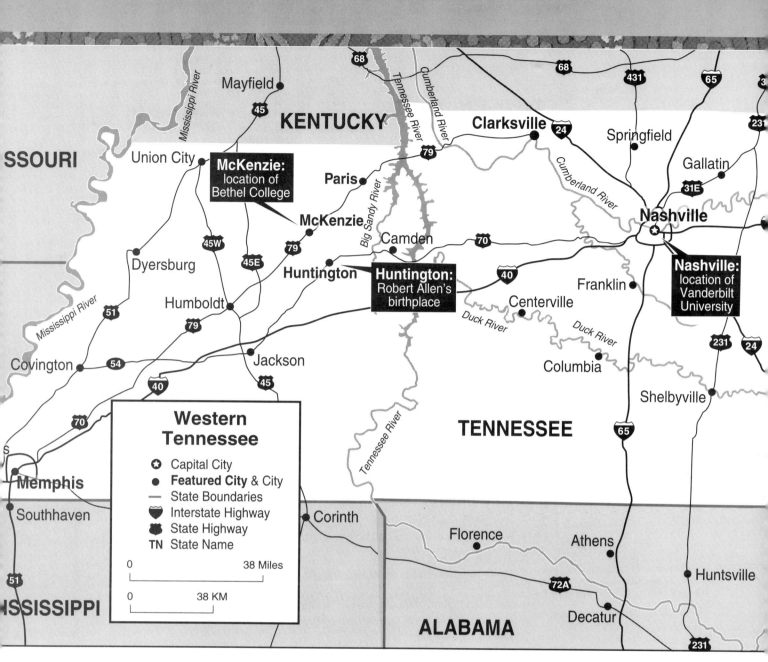

Map Work

1. About how far is McKenzie (where Bethel College is located) from Huntingdon (where Robert Allen was born)?

2. About how far are McKenzie and Huntingdon from Nashville (where Vanderbilt University is located)?

3. What states border Tennessee to the north, south, and west?

4. Robert Allen wants to drive from Nashville to the Mississippi River. What route should he take? Give directions.

5. Ask your classmates questions about the map. For example, *What river crosses western Tennessee?*

Taking Notes

Please complete the outline below with information from Reading 7.
Add more numbers and letters as you need them.

Robert Allen: Love of Learning

I. Childhood in Tennessee

    A. Raised by grandfather in mountains

        1. no schooling

        2. learned carpentry

    B.

II. First Classroom—Bethel College

III. Graduate School—Vanderbilt University

Exercise A: Using the Past Perfect Tense

The past perfect is used to talk about actions that happened before something else in the past. To form the past perfect, use:

had (simple past tense of *have*) + past participle of the verb

Complete the sentences with the past perfect tense of the verbs in parentheses.

> *Example:* Robert and his grandfather <u>had lived</u> in the mountains for many years before Robert went to school. (live)

1. Robert _____ carpentry before he knew how to read. (learn)

2. Before he started school, Robert _____ a living by making things from wood. (make)

3. Robert _____ himself to read before he met Claudine Halpers, the librarian. (teach)

4. Few people in town _____ the truth about Robert before the librarian told them. (know)

5. She _____ many times that Robert should take the GED before he finally took the test. (suggest)

6. Robert _____ the GED before he entered Bethel College. (pass)

7. The teachers _____ never _____ a person such as Robert before he walked into their classrooms. (see)

8. They _____ never _____ anyone speak like Robert before. (hear)

9. By the time Robert left Bethel College, he _____ A's in every subject except typing. (receive)

10. Robert _____ his doctorate's degree by the time he completed his eleventh year of school. (earn)

Exercise B: Combining Information

Read the sets of sentences below. Take the information from the second sentence and combine it with the first sentence. Write out the full sentence. (Caution: The information to be added does not always fit at the end of the sentence.) Use a comma in the first sentence to separate the information added from the second sentence.

> *Example*:   Robert Allen grew up in Huntingdon. Huntingdon is a rural community 90 miles west of Nashville.
> *Robert Allen grew up in Huntingdon, a rural community 90 miles west of Nashville.*

1. The first person to help Robert Allen was Claudine Halpers. Claudine Halpers was the county librarian.

    _____

    _____

2. She encouraged Robert to take the GED. The GED is the high school equivalency test.

    _____

    _____

3. After passing the GED, Robert entered Bethel College. Bethel College is a small, four-year college nearby.

    _____

    _____

4. Another person who helped Robert was Gene McMahan. Gene McMahan was one of Robert's teachers at Bethel.

    _____

    _____

5. Robert received a scholarship to Vanderbilt University. Vanderbilt University is located in Nashville, Tennessee.

    _____

    _____

6. Robert Allen shocked his teachers and classmates. Robert was dressed poorly.

    _____

    _____

7. After graduating, Robert thought about his future plan. His future plan was to get a job.

    _____

    _____

Exercise C: Connecting Ideas

The following words and phrases are often used to connect ideas between sentences:

As a result,	(RESULT/EFFECT)
In fact,	(EMPHASIS)
In other words,	(REPETITION)
Instead,	(ALTERNATIVE)
Nevertheless,	(CONTRAST)

Think about how the ideas in the sentences below are connected. Then, fill in the blanks with the correct connectors.

1. Robert Allen had never been in a classroom until he was 31 years old.

    _____, he had earned a doctorate in literature
    by the time he was 42.

2. Few people in Robert's community knew about his love of learning.

    _____, most people thought he was slow or
    stupid.

3. Robert's grandfather did not send him to school.

    _____, his grandfather taught him carpentry.

4. Robert read everything he could. _____, he
    read over 2,000 books he bought from yard sales.

5. The county librarian, Claudine Halpers, said that Robert read his way
    through the county library. _____, he actually
    read all the books on the shelves.

6. Robert had never seen even simple technology.

    _____, he did not even know how to use
    an elevator.

7. Robert did very well in his classes at Bethel College.

    _____, he received a scholarship to continue
    his studies at Vanderbilt University.

8. The farthest that Robert had ever traveled was Nashville.

    _____, he knew very little about the world
    around him.

Notes and Questions on Reading 7

Part A: Paragraphs

Reading 7 "paints a picture" of a person—Robert Allen. It does not tell everything about him, but it does tell a lot about one part of his life—his determination to learn. Think about the differences between the "portraits" of Robert Allen and Maya Lin (Reading 2). Which portrait do you prefer? Why?

Look at Reading 7 as introduction, body, and conclusion. Discuss the answers to these questions as you go:

1. In which paragraph do you first learn what is so important about Robert Allen's life?

2. How many paragraphs does the writer use to show that Robert Allen's life is "a lesson in determination"?

3. How does the final paragraph serve as part of the body? How does the final paragraph also serve as the conclusion?

Part B: Order

Because Reading 7 is about a person's life, you expect it to follow the order of time. Reading 7 follows a straight chronology even more than Reading 2.

Discuss the answers to the following questions to check the order of time:

1. In the reading, where does Robert Allen's life "begin"?

2. How does time move through the reading? What are the divisions of time? What does the writer stop to discuss along the way?

3. In which paragraph does the writer tell you about Robert Allen's first school experience?

4. In which paragraph does the writer bring you closest to the present time?

5. How does the selection end? At the end of Robert Allen's life? Do we know the outcome of his life?

Remember that writers often use chronological order to narrate and develop events through time.

Preliminary Writing

You and your teacher can decide which of the following activities to do. They will help prepare you for your own composition. Write either in your journal or in your notebook.

1. In your opinion, what is remarkable about Robert Allen? Write about it.

2. Make a list of people that you think are remarkable. Next to each name on your list, make some notes about what each person has done.

3. Imagine that you are Robert Allen. Write about learning to read. Use your imagination. Also write about other people's reactions to you. Remember that they think you are stupid.

4. As Robert Allen, write about your friend, Claudine Halpers. Use your imagination. Remember that she is the only person who really believes in you at a certain point in your life.

5. In your opinion, what makes a person's life "remarkable"? Write about your own idea of a "remarkable life." Give examples to support your ideas.

6. In the first paragraph of Reading 7, the writer says that parts of Robert Allen's life are "a lesson in determination." What does the writer mean? Write about why you think Robert Allen's life is "a lesson in determination."

Composition 7 (Biography)

Instructions for Composition 7

Please follow the instructions below. Work in pairs whenever possible, especially with numbers 2–3 and 5–7.

1. Think of a person whose life is different in some way. Choose a person whose life is "a lesson in something" (courage, determination, stupidity, goodness, patience, power, etc.). (Check the topics on the next page for ideas.) Who is your audience? (Who do you want to read your composition?) Who needs to learn the lesson of this person's life? Make a note of who your audience is.

2. Make a list of the details of this person's life. Choose details that show what the lesson is.

3. Go over your list. Cross out any details that don't illustrate your point. Add others that do, as they come to mind.

4. Write out a draft of your essay. Use Reading 7 as a model, if you wish.

5. After you finish writing, read over your draft. See if it paints a picture of the person as you see him or her. Check to see if all the details work together to complete your portrait. Make changes as you read and reread. Ask a classmate to read it and give you suggestions.

6. Check your draft against these questions:

   • Do you clearly introduce your reader to the most important quality of this person?

   • Do you include a lot of details to illustrate this quality?

   • Does your conclusion tell the reader more about the person?

7. Continue to make changes. When you are satisfied with your essay, proofread it.

   • Check the following: title, margins, indentations, capital letters, punctuation, and spelling.

8. Make corrections as you proofread. Then wait for your teacher's instructions.

Suggested Topics for Composition 7

Write about:

1. A person who overcame a great difficulty or handicap

2. A person whose actions showed great courage

3. A person who did something original

4. A person who sacrificed his or her life to save others

5. A person who inspired others by his or her actions

6. The person who has influenced your life the most

7. A person who accomplished something that others said could not be done

8. A person who did what she or he wanted to do even though other people did not approve

9. A person who will always be remembered for _____

10. A person who made it possible for others to achieve their goals

11. A person whose actions destroyed the lives of others

12. A person whose actions caused other people to lose their lives

13. A person whose life is a positive example for others

14. A person whom you will remember as long as you live

 # Connecting

Search the Internet for information on special awards or recognition given to remarkable people. You might choose an award such as the Nobel Prize, the Pulitzer Prize, the Congressional Medal of Honor, Olympic medals, or other awards you know about. Find out who gives the awards, when, and to whom. Share the information you find with a partner or with your class.

Describing a Procedure

HOME FOR SALE
BY APPOINTMENT
821-1000

FOR SALE
725-4514

Look at the photos and the ads.

- What is for sale and for rent?
- What do you know about the houses and apartments from the ads and the photos?
- Who do you think will buy the houses or rent the apartments?
- Are the prices low or high?

Reading 8

Buy—If You Can!

(1) It was a brand-new home. It cost $154,000. Sarah Jennings of Bay Shore, New York was ready to buy it, but her real estate agent suggested getting a home inspection. After four hours, the home inspector gave Jennings a list of over 20 problems with the "new" home. Jennings said, "I was just devastated… It was less than perfect." Since the problems were minor and would cost little to fix, Jennings decided to buy the house anyway. Many people are now adding the important step of home inspection into the process of buying a home.

(2) A home inspector does not check to see if the price is reasonable. The inspector checks on the building. Is it safe? Do the electricity and water work well? Is the roof in good condition? What repairs may be necessary? The inspector gives an estimate of the cost for putting the home in good working condition. If the home inspector finds serious problems, the buyer may want to consider looking for another house.

(3) After the inspection, Sarah Jennings made an offer on the house. Usually a buyer puts down some money (1–5% of the purchase price) to show intent to buy. The seller and buyer may need to negotiate before they decide on the price for the house. In Bay Shore, there are more buyers than houses. So Sarah paid full price and did not negotiate.

(4) Then she needed to get a mortgage, which is a loan for purchasing property. There are different types of loans available, and it's important to consider the interest rate, the required down payment, and other fees. Sarah filled out an application for a mortgage. Next, she also made a down payment, about 10% of the loan amount. The bank or lending agency checked her income, work history, bank accounts, credit history, the sales contract, and the property. The FHA (Federal Housing Administration) recommends that the monthly housing expenses should be no more than 29% of a family's income. The bank wanted to be sure that Sarah was able to afford the loan. It also wanted to make sure the house was worth the price. It took up to six weeks for the application process to be completed. Once the application was completed and approved, the final papers were prepared and a closing date arranged. After the closing, Sarah celebrated.

➡

(6)   Housing prices are increasing. Is there any help for middle-income and lower-income families? HUD (The U.S. Department of Housing and Urban Development) has a number of programs to help families find affordable housing. HUD owns homes in some areas and sells them at reasonable prices to lower-income families. The FHA (an agency in HUD) provides loans to those who need them. Other local agencies are working in communities to build more affordable housing and to help qualified people buy them.

The American dream of owning a home is still possible. But there are many people looking. In Bay Shore, NY recently, there were more than 2,000 people interested in buying 52 houses in a new housing project. Of those people, 1,948 families are still looking! But Sarah is not one of them.

NOTE: Information in Reading 8 is adapted from Randi Reigenbaum, "The Unaffordable Dream," *Newsday* (6 July 2000).

Vocabulary from Reading 8

Find these words in Reading 8. Examine the use of each word and guess its meaning. If you are not sure, ask a classmate or check your dictionary.

Nouns	Verbs	Adjectives
agent	approve	affordable
closing date	consider	brand-new
community	negotiate	devastated
condition	provide	local
contract	put down	lower-income
credit	recommend	middle-income
estimate		minor
expense		perfect
housing project		qualified
income		reasonable
inspection		required
inspector		safe
intent		serious
interest rate		suitable
lending agency		
mortgage		
offer		
process		
purchase price		
real estate		
repairs		

Vocabulary Work

Part 1

Use words from the vocabulary list on page 110 to fill in the blanks.

My friend found a wonderful house that she wants to buy. It's a small two-bedroom house. It's not far from here, so it's in the _____ area. The real estate agent wants her to _____ $800 on the house. There are some small problems. There's a _____ problem with a kitchen door. She got an _____ of about $100 to fix it. The rest of the house is in good _____ She will hear from the bank next week. The _____ is $80,000. My friend thinks it's _____, and the _____ is about 9% right now. I hope she gets it.

Part 2

Work in pairs to match the words below with their meanings.

_____ 1. recommend   **a.** to talk with others and come to an agreement

_____ 2. provide   **b.** a guess about an amount

_____ 3. negotiate   **c.** to think carefully about something

_____ 4. consider   **d.** a written agreement

_____ 5. estimate   **e.** an examination or review of something

_____ 6. expense   **f.** money received from work

_____ 7. contract   **g.** to advise or to suggest something

_____ 8. inspection   **h.** something you spend money on

_____ 9. income   **i.** to give

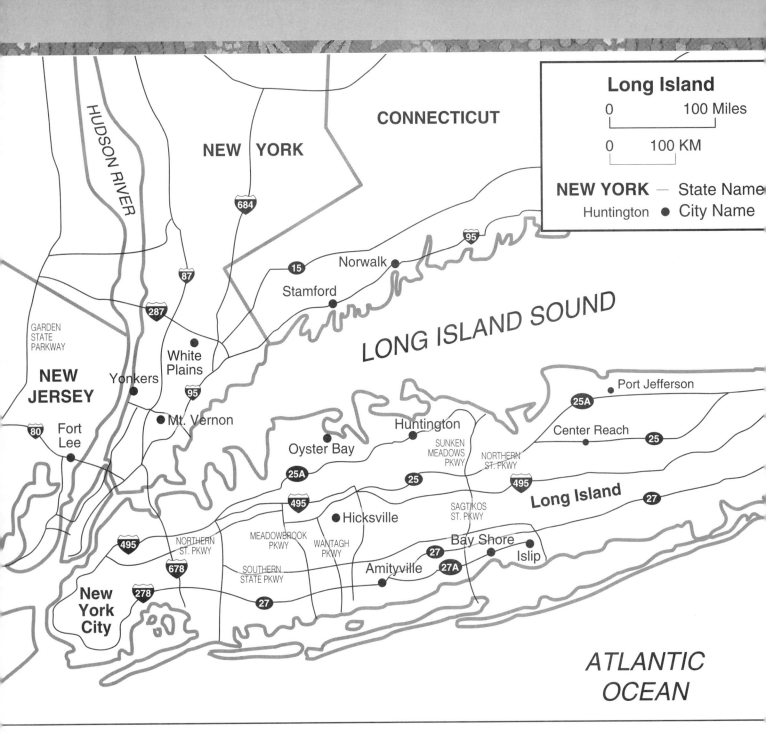

Map Work

1. Where is Long Island? In what state?

2. About how far is Islip from Amityville? What route can you take for this trip?

3. Where is Huntington? How far is it from Amityville?

4. In what direction do you travel to go to New York City from Islip?

5. Ask your classmates questions about the map.

Taking Notes

Please complete the outline below with information from Reading 8. Add more numbers and letters as you need them.

Steps in Buying a House		
1. Inspect _____ _____ _____ 2. _____ _____ _____	3. _____ _____ _____ 4. _____ _____ _____	5. _____ _____ _____ 6. _____ _____ _____

What the Bank or Lending Agency Needs
1.
2.
3.
4.
5.

Agencies to Help People Buy Homes	
Name of Agency	How It Can Help
HUD	
FHA	

Exercise A: Capitalizing

The sentences below are not correct. Capital letters are missing. Please change the lowercase letters to capital letters where necessary.

1. sara jennings was ready to buy a brand-new house.

2. she went to see an apartment in islip, new york with her friends, mary and james.

3. hud, the u.s. department of housing and urban development, has programs to help families find housing.

4. the jennings family was able to get a loan from the federal housing administration.

5. a housing inspector named dan nelson says that the inspections often save buyers a lot of money.

6. the dime savings bank offers a variety of loans and mortgages.

7. the new housing project, the long island housing partnership's southwind village, had 52 houses for sale.

8. there were more than 2,000 people in the bay shore area of new york who applied for the houses.

9. many families like the richardsons have moved to huntington or other towns on long island.

10. last march, the rent increased from $1,100 to $1,500.

Exercise B: Using Articles

Fill in the blanks below with the indefinite article *a (an)* or the definite article *the.* Remember that *the* identifies something or someone definite. If you can answer the question *which one?* use *the.* Use *a* or *an* to talk about a nonspecific thing. Use *an* before nouns that start with a vowel sound. Use *a* before other nouns.

1. Sarah Jennings bought _____ new home for $154,000.

2. _____ home inspector found 20 small problems with _____ new home.

3. He found _____ problem with _____ front door of _____ house.

4. _____ inspector gave _____ estimate for fixing it.

5. _____ Jennings family was looking for _____ new home for three months.

6. _____ FHA (_____ agency in HUD) can provide loans to help people buy houses.

7. _____ American dream of owning _____ home is still possible.

8. Sarah Jennings needed to get _____ mortgage from _____ bank.

9. _____ bank was offering _____ interest rate of 7%.

10. For Sarah, _____ application process took only three weeks, but it can take longer to get _____ mortgage approved.

Exercise C: Using Complex Sentences to Synthesize Ideas

Answer the questions below from your understanding of Reading 8.

Think about how the ideas in the sentences below are connected. Then, use the connector in parentheses to combine the sentences.

1. Sarah Jennings was lucky. She got her new home. (because)

   _____

   _____

2. The FHA recommends things. The monthly housing expenses should be no more than 29% of a person's income. (that)

   _____

   _____

3. Sarah's friends, Mary and James, need to move. They check the newspapers for ads. (so)

   _____

   _____

4. There are some housing projects in Huntington. The projects may offer some possibilities for Mary and James. (that)

   _____

   _____

5. A person finds a suitable home. They have it inspected. (when)

   _____

   _____

6. The buyer fills out a mortgage application. The bank checks the information and makes a decision. (after)

   _____

   _____

7. The FHA gives loans. The people can buy homes. (so that)

   _____

   _____

8. People often have their homes inspected. They buy the homes. (before)

   _____

   _____

Notes and Questions on Reading 8

Part A: Paragraphs

Reading 8 explains a procedure: what generally happens when a person buys a home.

Look at Reading 8 as introduction, body, and conclusion. Work through the following questions to make sure you see the writer's plan:

1. In which paragraph does the writer really introduce the subject of the essay? Why do you think the writer begins the essay by telling you about Sarah Jennings?

2. Which paragraphs form the body of the essay? How does the first paragraph prepare the reader for the rest of the body?

3. How does the writer conclude the essay? Is this an effective conclusion? Can you think of other ways to conclude the essay?

Part B: Order

Now go back through Reading 8 and check the writer's way of organizing the content:

1. Locate the events that occur before a buyer goes to a bank for a loan. What words and structures does the writer use to make the order of events clear?

2. Locate the procedure that the bank requires buyers to follow.

The writer follows a basic time order—*chronological* order. Since most people understand procedures as steps in time, this seems logical.

Preliminary Writing

You and your teacher can decide which of the following activities to do. They will help prepare you for your own composition. Write in your journal or in your notebook.

1. Write about the advantages of owning a home. Why do people want their own homes? How does it make people feel? How does it affect them socially? Why do some people prefer owning to renting?

2. Create an imaginary time line for a family who is looking for a place. Continue until they move to a new place. Identify each "step" in your time line.

3. Write out the procedure that you and your family went through to find a place to live (your current home or another place).

4. Make a list of some of the most complex procedures you have ever followed: getting admitted to a school? Being treated for a medical problem? Getting a car registered? Getting a marriage license? Graduating from school?

Composition 8 (Process Description)

Instructions for Composition 8

Please follow the instructions below. Work in pairs whenever possible, especially with numbers 2–3 and 5–6.

1. Think of a procedure that you want to write about. (Check the suggested topics on the following page if you need ideas.) Choose as your audience a group of people who need to understand the procedure. Who are these people? Why do they need to understand the procedure?

2. Make a list of words and phrases that come to mind as you think of the steps in this procedure.

3. Note a word or two that shows how you feel about the procedure. Do you want to show that it is easy? Difficult? Fun? Exciting?

4. Write out a draft of your composition. Check back to Reading 8 if you want to use it as a model for your writing. Read over your writing several times to make sure it says what you want it to say. Make changes until you are satisfied.

5. Check your draft against these questions:

   • Does your introduction sound interesting? Does it introduce the procedure you will write about?

   • Do you clearly explain the procedure? Do you include a lot of details?

   • Do you give your reader a reason to care about the topic?

   • Do you conclude with something interesting to the reader?

6. Make changes as you read and reread your essay. Ask a classmate to read it and make suggestions.

7. When you are satisfied with your changes, proofread your writing.

   • Check the following: title, margins, spelling, capital letters, grammar, punctuation, and indentation of paragraphs.

Make corrections where needed. Then, follow your teacher's instructions.

Suggested Topics for Composition 8

Describe and explain the following procedures:

1. getting a loan from a bank to buy a car

2. choosing a person to marry

3. getting married in your culture or religion

4. dying and being buried or cremated in your culture or religion

5. taking someone out on a date

6. buying an important home appliance (a washing machine, a computer, etc.)

7. getting a divorce

8. becoming a winning chess player, tennis player, etc.

9. doing a particular scientific experiment

10. preparing your favorite food

11. cheering up a friend who is very sad

12. using a particular machine (you decide which one)

13. having a pleasant conversation with a member of the opposite sex

14. having a (family) meeting

15. resolving a legal problem over property, damages, or an unpaid loan

 # Connecting

Search the Internet for information on real estate, loan/mortgage companies, and agencies that do home inspections. Find out what prices and rates are in your local area. Share the information you find with a partner or with your class.

Unit 9 Defining

Composition Focus: Expanded Definition

Organizational Focus: Partition

Grammatical Focus: Complex Sentences
Gerunds and Infinitives

Look at the photos.

● What do you see?

● What do the photos have in common? What is similar about all the photos?

● How is each one different? What is different about all the photos?

● What do you think you will read about?

● What are some important words to describe the people and relationships
in the photos?

Reading 9

NOTE : Reading 9 has two parts. In Part I, you will "hear" one person's opinion. In Part II, you will "hear" another opinion. The two writers disagree. They have different ideas. Read both parts and discuss the disagreement with your classmates.

I
What's in a Word?

(1) Some words are more difficult than others to explain or define. Some are hard to define because we have strong feelings about them. We have strong emotions about words such as *divorce* or *childhood*. We may feel sad, happy, or angry when we think about these words. Our own experiences affect the way we feel about the words. Definitions of other words have changed as people and the world have changed. Traditionally, the word *mother* meant both female parent *and* primary caregiver (the person who cares for the children). The word *father* meant both male parent *and* breadwinner (the person who earns money for the family). If there was a "mother," then usually there was a "father." In general, this is still true, but two points of this traditional definition are changing.

(2) There is a growing number of single women who want to be mothers. They have not included a man, or "father," in their plans. These women are choosing to have babies and raise them alone. They are not widows or divorcées. They are mostly women with good jobs. They are economically independent. They are in their late 30s, and they have never found "Mr. Right" (a man they would like to marry). "I decided I wasn't going to turn 40 without at least exploring the possibility of having a child," explains Marianne Boswell, a single mother living in the Boston area. "I wanted it to be a conscious decision, as opposed to something that just didn't happen to me."

(3) These women become mothers in different ways. Some adopt a baby. Some carefully choose a partner. Others choose donor insemination, a medical process that can cause pregnancy. The National Center for Health Statistics reports that 32% of all births are now to unmarried women. In 1960, the rate was only 5.3%. After two years of carefully thinking about the decision, Marianne chose to adopt and now has a beautiful little boy.

(4) There is another group that is

also questioning the traditional definitions. In this group are men who choose to stay at home and care for their children. They, not their wives, are the primary caregivers. As Randall Mitchell says in the movie "Mr. Mom," "When my daughter wakes up at night, she calls for her daddy." This untraditional parent thinks he is lucky. He has an experience that most men never have.

Mitchell's wife agrees, although she was unsure at first about changing her role from caregiver to breadwinner.

(5)   As society changes, our definitions change. People redefine themselves and their family relationships. As a result, we may need to create some new words. Somehow, "single mother" and "Mr. Mom" do not seem like very good names.

II
What's in a Word?
An Opposing View

(1) Yes, the definition of *mother* has changed for some women, but not for all. There are still many women who believe in the traditional family. A child needs two parents, both a mother *and* a father. *Motherhood* does not work without *fatherhood*.

(2)   Women are having children alone, but they are thinking only of themselves. They are not thinking about the children. Some studies have shown that children of single mothers have more problems in school than children of two-parent families. Being a single parent is not easy. It is very expensive. Many women have to change work or find extra jobs to support themselves and their children. It is tiring and stressful for single parents. So how can it be good for their children?

(3)   Everyone wants to feel loved. But the answer is not to have children to fill the empty place in one's own life. Children should be born to two mature adults who can take care of them. Children need parents who will love them, not *own* them or *use* them. The word *mother* means *giving*. It does not mean *taking* or *using*. The same is true of the word *father*.

Vocabulary from Reading 9

Find these words in Reading 9. Examine the use of each word and guess its meaning. If you are not sure, ask a classmate or check your dictionary.

Nouns
breadwinner
caregiver
childhood
divorce
divorcée
donor insemination
emotion
fatherhood
motherhood
partner
relationship
role
widow
wife (wives)

Verbs
affect
choose
explore
redefine
support

Adverbs
economically
traditionally

Adjectives
conscious
lucky
mature
primary
single
stressful
unmarried
unsure
untraditional

Other
opposed to

Vocabulary Work

Part 1

Match the words below with their meanings.

_____ 1. affect   a. to select; to pick something

_____ 2. choose   b. to bring up; to take care of (a child)

_____ 3. explore   c. adult; fully grown

_____ 4. raise   d. first or most important

_____ 5. stressful   e. to cause something to change

_____ 6. mature   f. against; proving the opposite side

_____ 7. primary   g. to examine or search carefully

_____ 8. opposed to   h. to provide money or things needed by others

_____ 9. conscious   i. causing worries or problems

_____ 10. support   j. thoughtful; full of understanding

Part 2

Answer these questions using the vocabulary list on page 124. Work in pairs.

1. Which words in the list on page 124 are about *family*? Write them down.

2. What is another word for *feelings*?

3. Which words describe a person who is not married?

4. Which word can describe a person who wins $10,000?

5. Which word means *not certain*?

6. What word describes something that is not usual or customary in a culture?

Make up other questions about the words on the list to ask your partner.

Taking Notes

Please complete the outline below with information from Reading 9 (I).

Defining the Words "mother" and "father"

I. Traditional definition

    A. mother: female parent and _____

    B. father: _____

II. Challenges to traditional definition

    A. mother: _____ women who have

           _____ and raise them alone

        1. adopt a child

        2. _____

        3. _____

    B. father: men who _____

        _____

Exercise A: Using Infinitives and Gerunds

Gerunds and infinitives are formed from verbs.

gerund = verb + *-ing*
infinitives = *to* + verb

Some verbs are usually followed by gerunds (such as *enjoy, finish, quit, suggest*). Other verbs are often followed by infinitives (such as *agree, choose, decide, hope, plan, want*). Some expressions are usually followed by gerunds (such as: *tired of, enough of, worried about, sorry about, interested in*). (See Appendix B for a more complete list.)

Read the sentences below. Choose the correct form to complete each sentence.

1. Many single women want (to be / being) mothers.

2. Marianne was interested in (to explore / exploring) the possibilities.

3. After two years, she decided (to have / having) a baby alone.

4. Some people believe that a mother is not enough for (to raise / raising) a child.

5. Some men choose (to stay / staying) home to take care of the children.

6. Many of them enjoy (to take / taking) care of the children.

7. Sometimes their wives are worried about (to change / changing) roles.

8. Some women need (to change / changing) jobs to support their families.

9. Others feel sorry about (to leave / leaving) their children while they go to work.

10. We probably need (to create / creating) some words for these new family roles.

Exercise B: Connecting Ideas

Complete the sentences below with the following *connecting words.* Think about the meaning as you decide. You may need to use some connectors more than once.

after	*and*	*because*	*that*
although	*as*	*but*	*when*

1. Some words change in definition _____ people in a society change.

2. Some women choose to have children _____ they have no husbands.

3. One woman said _____ she wanted to think carefully about having a child.

4. Women who choose to have children alone are usually economically independent _____ are in their late 30s.

5. One woman who chose to have a child alone said _____ it was very difficult for her.

6. One man decided to stay at home with his new baby _____ he wanted the experience of taking care of her.

7. He wanted to stay at home with his child, _____ his boss and co-workers thought he was crazy.

8. Now, his young daughter calls for her daddy _____ she wakes up at night.

9. He plans to return to work _____ his daughter's first birthday.

10. _____ people and society change, our definitions may need to change.

Exercise C: Writing Complex Sentences

Read the questions below and study the partial answers. Please complete the answers according to the ideas/information from Reading 9. Your answers do not need to be word-for-word from the reading.

1. Why are words such as *divorce* and *childhood* so hard to define?
   They are so difficult to define because...

2. How is the word *mother* traditionally defined?
   It is traditionally defined as the parent who...

3. Which women have not included a father in their plans for motherhood?
   They are mostly women who...

4. How do these women become mothers?
   Some adopt children, while...

5. How do these single women feel about their roles?
   They say that...

6. Which men are questioning the traditional definitions of *mother* and *father*?
   They are men who...

7. Why does one untraditional father think he is lucky?
   He thinks he is lucky because...

8. How might the wife of an untraditional father feel?
   She might feel that...

Notes and Questions on Reading 9

Part A: Paragraphs

Reading 9 (I) is an *analysis by definition*. The writer presents her ideas by defining a word (including all the meanings of that word) and by explaining how the definition is changing. We call it a definition, but it is much more, of course.

Look at Reading 9 (I) as introduction, body, and conclusion. Work through the following questions to make sure that you see the writer's plan:

1. What movement happens during the introduction? How does the writer present the "real" topic? Where does the writer tell you her plan for developing the topic?

2. How is the body developed? Are the "two points" treated equally?

3. The conclusion is very short. Is it too short? If your answer is yes, what would you do to make it fuller?

Look at Reading 9 (II). It is called an "opposing view." What is the writer opposing? Does the writer oppose everything in (I)?

Look at the three paragraphs in 9 (II). What does the writer do in the first paragraph? In the second paragraph? How does the writer conclude in the last paragraph?

Part B: Order

The writer of Reading 9 (I) is defining the word *mother* by explaining traditional and nontraditional meanings of *mother* and *father*. Go back to 9 (I) and check the writer's way of organizing the content:

1. Find the traditional definitions of *mother* and *father*.

2. What follows the traditional definitions?

3. Which "pieces" of the traditional definitions are being redefined these days? Explain. (As you saw in Reading 4, a writer can analyze a subject by examining its parts—aspects, reasons, etc. This method of developing an essay is called *partition*, meaning "to divide into parts.")

The writer of Reading 9 (II) defines the word *mother* differently. She is writing in response to the writer of 9 (I). How do you know that 9 (II) is a response? To which part of 9 (I) does 9 (II) respond? See how 9 (II) is organized by answering these questions:

1. Where does the writer of 9 (II) state her point of disagreement?

2. Where does the writer of 9 (II) explain the problem, as she sees it? How does she explain it?

3. Where and how does the writer close her discussion? (Whom do you agree with, the writer of 9 (I) or 9 (II)?)

Preliminary Writing

You and your teacher can decide which of the following activities to do. They will help prepare you for your own composition. Write either in your journal or notebook.

1. Make a list of words that you think are difficult to define (like "mother"). Look over your list. Circle those about which you think you and your classmates would disagree *the most*. Try to state what is so difficult about them.

2. Write out your own definition of "mother." (You do not need to agree with the writers of Reading 9.) Write out a definition of "good mother." Are your two definitions different or the same? Do the same for "father" and "good father." Are your definitions different?

3. Think about your own culture. Is there a point of general disagreement between people of your age and the people of your parents' (or grandparents') age? Is it a matter of definition?

4. Describe the different definitions. (Of course these definitions show different values and experience, don't they?)

5. Write about a point of difference between men and women. Is it a matter of definition? Try to define this point or idea as you think (some) men do. Define it as you think (some) women do.

6. Write about a word/concept whose definition has changed for *you*. How *did* you define it? How do you define it *now*? What has caused you to change your thinking? Being older? A particular experience? Write about this change.

7. Make a list of the words that you think will cause disagreements between you and your (future) children. What do you think the differences will be? How do you think your children will define some of these words? How will you define them as you get older?

8. Reread Parts I and II of Reading. What does the writer of Part II try to prove? Write a paragraph, stating the disagreement between the points of view in Parts I and II. Add your own point of view.

Composition 9 (Expanded Definition)

Instructions for Composition 9

Please follow the instructions below. Work in pairs whenever possible, especially with numbers 2–3 and 6–7.

1. Think of a word that you want to define. (Check the suggestions that follow if you need ideas.) It should be a word about which people have strong feelings, memories, or connections. Who is your audience? Who needs to read your definitions? (Are you going to write for people who will agree or disagree with you?)

2. Note all the words and phrases that come to mind when you think of about this word. Add comments, facts, figures, etc.—anything connected with the word.

3. Go over your list. Circle the things you want to use in your composition. Add other ideas that come to mind.

4. Write out a draft of your composition. Use Reading 9 as a model if you wish. Begin with a generally accepted or traditional definition. Then show how you/others define this word differently, or show how the definition is changing. Perhaps you want to show how your own definition has changed.

5. After you finish writing, go over your draft. See if it says what you want it to say. Make changes where necessary.

6. Next, check your draft against these questions:

   • Can your reader clearly understand *what* you are defining?

   • Do you make clear what you are doing with the definition? Are you showing how it has changed? Are you showing how *you* have changed? Are you showing how your culture is changing?

   • Do you illustrate with specific details, comments, statistics, and/or experiences?

   • After reading, will the reader understand the word you are defining in a fuller, deeper way? Will your writing make the reader think?

7. Continue to make changes as you read and reread your composition. Ask a classmate to read it and tell you if everything is clear. When you have made all the changes you want to make, proofread your essay.

   • Check the following: title, margins, indentation of paragraphs, capital letters, punctuation, and spelling.

Make any necessary corrections as you proofread. Then, follow your teacher's instructions.

Suggested Topics for Composition 9

Choose one of the following words and explain what it means to you, to others, or both:

1. home
2. wife
3. husband
4. ancestor
5. daughter *or* son
6. money
7. success
8. discrimination
9. teenager
10. secret
11. traditions
12. wedding *or* marriage
13. divorce
14. criticism

Connecting

Search the Internet for information on parent groups or organizations that give support to single parents, house-husbands, or other non-traditional family situations. Find out if there are any such groups in your area. What types of help or information do they give? Share the information you find with a partner or with your class.

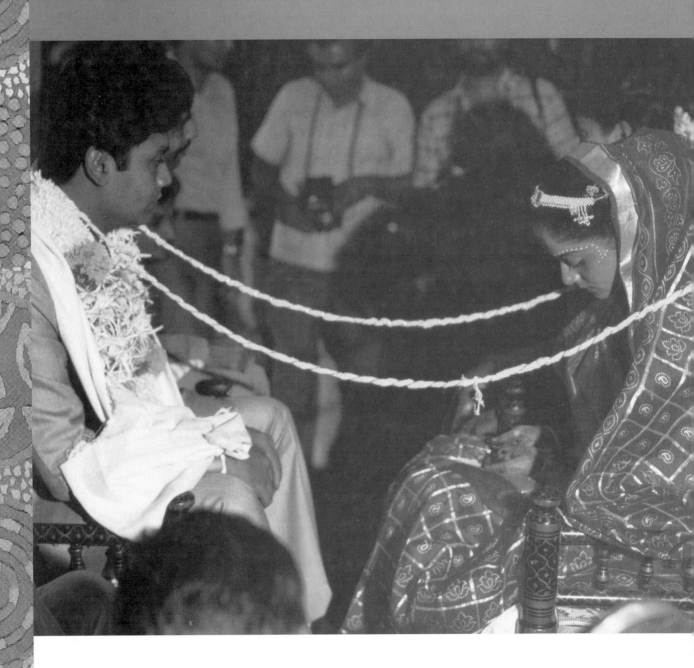

In this Indian wedding ceremony, a cord is placed around
the necks of the couple to protect them from bad luck.

 Composition Focus: Analysis

 Organizational Focus: Induction

 Grammatical Focus: Passive Voice

These men are in prison in
Brazil for human rights abuses.

Look at the photos.

- What do you see?
- What do you think you will read about?
- What important words describe the people and places in the photos?

Reading 10

NOTE: Reading 10 has two parts. Part II is an addition to Part I, not an opposing view (as in Unit 9). The general subject of both parts is human rights, although both are specifically about women. The setting in 10 (I) is Brazil and in 10 (II) is India, but human rights violations take place all over the world. The writer is *not* saying that human rights violations happen only in those two countries.

I
Crimes of Passion

(1) A man in Brazil killed his wife. He was arrested and there was a trial. He was given one year in prison, and now he's back on the street. How can that be? Sadly, the laws were not working. Women are abused or killed each year by their spouses or boyfriends in Brazil and many of these crimes are not reported. Women know that most men are never convicted of these crimes. Human rights groups all over Brazil are trying to change the system, but it is not just the laws and courts that need to be changed. It's the attitude of people and of society that also needs to change.

(2) The man said that *she* was seeing someone else. He was protecting his honor. In fact, "defense of honor" is popular in Brazilian courts. In some areas of Brazil, this works in about 80% of this kind of court case. When a man is seeing another woman, it is a different story.

(3) Some changes are happening. Recently, a man was given 19 years in prison for killing his wife. This gives hope to human rights groups. However, the situation is still not good in Brazil. In fact, it is far from ideal in many countries.

II
Crimes of Greed

(1) In some parts of India, the family of a bride gives money and gifts to the groom before a marriage. They are paying for the support and care that the groom will give their daughter in the future. If the groom is an office clerk, the bride's family might pay $5,000. If he is an engineer, the family might pay $50,000. This payment is called a *dowry*.

(2) In recent years, dowries have made people greedy. The groom or his family wants more—more money, more appliances. He asks for more. Maybe the bride's family is slow in paying the dowry. Maybe the groom decides that he needs even more money. Then what happens? He abuses or even kills his spouse. If he kills her, he is free to remarry and get another dowry. Human rights groups in India call these *dowry deaths*. This means killing a bride because she does not bring enough money to the marriage.

(3) It sounds terrible, and the number of dowry deaths is increasing. Why? Women in Indian society have a low position. They are not as important as men. They do not have the same rights. At the same time, people want to buy more things. For some people, the dowry system has become an easy way to get more, to have more, to be successful. In India, there were more than 5,800 dowry deaths reported in one year. There were probably many more. The police are slow to check these types of cases. Even when they do check, they are likely to say the death was an accident.

(4) Unfortunately, less than 1% of these cases end with punishment or prison. Fortunately, there are now some educated men who do not take a dowry, but the dowry custom is hard to stop.

Vocabulary from Reading 10

Find these words in Reading 10. Examine the use of each word and guess its meaning. If you are not sure, ask a classmate or check your dictionary.

Nouns
appliance
attitude
bride
case
court
crime
defense
dowry
greed
groom
honor
human rights
law
lawyer
marriage
passion
payment
position
prison
punishment
society
spouse
trial
violation

Verbs
abuse
arrest
convict
protect
remarry

Adverbs
specifically
unfortunately

Adjectives
greedy
ideal
recent

Vocabulary Work

Part 1

Write these words in the proper categories.

arrest   marriage   trial   convict
prison   bride   court   dowry
protect   abuse   groom

Families and Weddings	Law and Punishment	
1. _____	1. _____	5. _____
2. _____	2. _____	6. _____
3. _____	3. _____	7. _____
4. _____	4. _____	

Part 2

Answer these questions using the vocabulary list on page 138. Work in pairs.

1. What is another word for *perfect*?

2. Generally, what are televisions, washing machines, stoves, and refrigerators?

3. What is breaking a law called?

4. Which word means *basic things that all people should have by law*?

5. What do you call *people living in a community*?

6. What is another word that means *to guard or keep away from danger*?

7. Which word describes a person who wants more without caring about others?

Make up other questions about the words on the list to ask your partner.

Taking Notes

Please complete the chart below with information from Reading 10 (I and II). The numbers in the columns correspond to the readings.

Crimes Against Women		
	I	II
Type of crime:	"crime of _____"	"crime of _____"
Reason for crime:	Man defending his _____	_____
Attitude of others:	_____	_____
Country discussed:	_____	India

Exercise A: Using Passive Voice

Look at the two sentences below. Both sentences give the same basic information. In the passive sentence, the dowry receives the action. In the passive, the receiver is considered more important than the cause.

Active: The family of the bride gives a dowry to the groom.

Passive: The groom is given a dowry (by the family of the bride).

To form simple passive sentences, you use:

be (is/are, was/were) + the past participle of the main verb

OR

modal + *be* + the past participle of the main verb

Complete the sentences below with past or present passive forms of the verbs in parentheses.

1. In many places, women _____ (kill) each year by their husbands.

2. Many cases _____ (not...report).

3. Most of the men _____ (never...convict) of these crimes.

4. In one case, a man _____ (arrest) and he _____ (give) only one year in prison.

5. If a woman kills her husband, she _____ (give) 10–20 years in prison.

6. Recently, a man in Brazil _____ (put) in prison for nineteen years for killing his wife.

7. According to custom, the bride's family gives money and gifts to the groom. This payment _____ (call) a dowry.

8. Some women in India _____ (killed) by their husbands because they do not bring enough money to the marriage.

Exercise B: Recognizing Elements of Cohesion

As we read, we use the information from one phrase or sentence to understand the next. Read these sentences and examine how sentences are carried forward. Then answer the questions about the italicized words below.

1. In Brazil, a number of women are killed each year by their husbands or boyfriends. These men say they are protecting *their* honor.

   Whose honor are these men protecting?

   _____

2. Recently, a man in Brazil was given 19 years in prison for killing his wife. *This* gives hope to human rights groups.

   What gives hope to human rights groups?

   _____

3. Brazilian human rights groups hope that the old attitudes are changing. The *situation* is far from ideal, however.

   What is the situation (in the *whole* reading)?

   _____

4. By custom, the bride's family gives money and gifts to the groom according to *his* position and job.

   According to whose position and job are gifts given?

   _____

5. By custom, the bride's family gives money and gifts to the groom. *The payment* is called a dowry.

   What payment is called a dowry?

   _____

6. If the bride's family is slow in paying or the groom decides that he needs more money, he might kill his wife. Human rights groups call *these* "dowry deaths."

   What do human rights groups call "dowry deaths"?

   _____

Exercise C: Using Different Verb Forms

Complete each sentence below by changing the verb(s) in parentheses to fit the grammar and time of the sentence.

1. In Brazil today, human rights groups _____ (try / are trying / tried) to change the justice system.

2. In Brazil, a man charged with killing his wife may say that she _____ (sees / was seeing) some other man.

3. A few months ago, a man in Brazil was sentenced to prison for _____ (killed / killing / kill) his wife.

4. The prison sentence _____ (gives / gave / will give) some hope to human rights groups.

5. They hope that the old ways _____ (changed / are changing / change).

6. Earlier this week, a newspaper again _____ (report / reporting / reported) that a man _____ (kill / killing / killed) his wife.

7. By custom, the family of a bride _____ (gives / is giving / gave) money and gifts to the groom.

8. In recent years, dowries have _____ (becoming / became / become) an easy way for greedy people to get money.

9. When the police do check the cases, they are likely to say the death _____ (was / is / will be) an accident.

10. Unfortunately, less than 1% of the cases _____ (ended / end / are ending) with punishment or prison.

Notes and Questions on Reading 10

Part A: Paragraphs

Reading 10 (I and II) is an analysis. It separates the subject in order to identify and explain it. Both essays analyze (examine in detail) certain feelings and attitudes toward women in two countries—Brazil and India. These analyses do not mean that everyone in those countries feels the same way toward women. No analysis is true for everyone or every place.

Look at both essays to see how the writer introduces, develops, and concludes the subject. Work through these questions:

1. In the first essay, how does the writer introduce the subject? What is the subject? Does the writer give it a name?

2. What happens in the second paragraph of the first essay?

3. How does the writer end the first essay? How important are the details in the conclusion?

4. In the second essay, how long does it take the writer to completely introduce the subject? Pick out one or two sentences in the first two paragraphs that are the most important in introducing the subject.

5. How does the writer develop the subject in the third paragraph of the second essay?

6. How does the writer conclude the second essay? What is similar about the two conclusions?

Part B: Order

The writer of both essays in Reading 10 presents many details to make readers believe the generalization: *The attitude of some societies toward women is such that women can lose their right to live.* Go back through Reading 10 to check how the writer arranged the details.

1. In which paragraph of the first essay does the writer first give details? In which paragraph does the writer explain the social attitude toward women? Does the writer ever state her generalization directly? How do you know what it is...or do you?

2. In which paragraph of the second essay does the writer first give details? Go through the rest of the essay and locate other details. How do you know the writer's generalization (her *thesis*)? Can you find it in a single sentence?

3. In both essays, find places where the writer says that negative attitudes toward women affect the court system, the police, etc. Does the writer make that statement directly or indirectly?

Both essays contain mostly details. The writer is analyzing (examining) a problem by giving shocking details. From them, the reader begins to understand the writer's generalization. It is not directly stated. This method of ordering ideas—organizing many details to illustrate a generalization—is called *induction*. You also saw this in Unit 6.

Preliminary Writing

You and your teacher can decide which of the following activities to do. They will help prepare you for your own composition. Write either in your journal or in your notebook.

1. What do the two readings in Unit 10 have in common? Write about their similarities.

2. Make a list of social customs that you think are not good in your own culture. These customs may not result in death, but you think they are negative or bad. If they do not have a name, then define or describe them.

3. Briefly analyze social "rules" for husbands and wives in your culture. Whom may husbands see? Whom may wives see? May wives go out or socialize without their husbands? Husbands without their wives? Explain.

4. Briefly tell what you remember most from "Crimes of Passion." Write about it in your own words.

5. Briefly tell what you remember most from "Crimes of Greed." Write about it in your own words.

6. Briefly analyze what families are supposed to do in a marriage in your culture or religion. What is the bride's family supposed to do? What is the groom's family supposed to do? Tell if they do these things before, during, or after the wedding ceremony.

Composition 10 (Analysis)

Instructions for Composition 10

Please follow the instructions below. Work in pairs whenever possible, especially with numbers 2–3 and 5–7.

1. Think of a situation or event in your culture that you want to analyze. Analyze the attitudes, customs, or rituals. It does not need to be something bad or negative, as in Reading 10. (Check the suggestions that follow if you need ideas.) Decide who your readers are. Do you want people who know nothing about your culture to read this? It's up to you, but you need to decide before you begin.

2. Write down words and phrases that come to mind as you think of this situation or event. Add examples, illustrations, facts, and figures as you think of them.

3. Go over your list. Circle those that you think you want to include in your composition. Add others as they come to mind.

4. Write out a draft of your composition. Check back to Reading 10 if you want to see how the writer works in details to develop the whole composition.

5. After you finish writing, go over your draft. See if it says what you want it to say. Make changes where necessary. Ask a classmate to read it and give you suggestions.

6. Next, check your draft against these questions:

   • Is your subject clear? Does your reader know what you are analyzing?

   • Do you include enough details to help your reader understand? Are all of your details important to your subject?

   • Is your composition interesting? Can it keep your reader's attention?

7. Continue to make changes as you read and reread your composition. When you are satisfied with what it says, proofread it.

   • Check the following: title, margins, indentation, capital letters, punctuation, and spelling.

Make any necessary changes as you proofread. Then, follow your teacher's instructions.

Suggested Topics for Composition 10

1. Analyze your cultural or religious traditions for the birth of a first child. What is the role of the paternal grandparents? The maternal grandparents? Does it make a difference if the child is a girl or a boy?

2. Analyze marriage customs in your culture. For example, is the marriage arranged by the parents? Do the parents visit each other before the wedding?

3. Analyze the attitudes, customs, and traditions for academic success (university graduation, graduation from medical school, etc.). For example, do the parents announce the event? Is there a special ceremony?

4. Analyze dating in your culture or religion. For example, is there dating? Is there a chaperone? Where may the unmarried couple go? May the girl see the boy alone?

5. According to your culture or religion, analyze women and work. For example, may a woman work outside the home? What jobs may she have? What do men think about their wives working? Who takes care of the children? Can she make more money than her husband?

6. Analyze the role of a student in your culture. How must a student behave? What are a family's obligations? Who pays the student's expenses? Explain.

7. Analyze social invitations in your culture. For example, who invites? Who accepts? Does the invited person take a gift? Does the invited person have to "return" the invitation?

8. Analyze the rules for conversation in your culture. For example, who can begin a conversation? Do the people talking to each other make eye contact? In casual conversation, what may people (not) talk about? Are there different "rules" for men and women? How are conversations "closed"? Do people shake hands when they leave?

9. Analyze driving in your culture. For example, who may drive? May women drive alone? Do parents let teenage children drive? Do people honk at each other? What does honking "mean"? Are drivers aggressive?

10. Analyze the roles of mothers and fathers of young children in your culture. For example, who changes diapers? Who feeds the children?

 # Connecting

Search the Internet for information on organizations and agencies that offer help related to spousal abuse. Are there service providers in your local area? What type of help do they offer wives and/or husbands? How can people contact these places? Share the information you find with a partner or with your class.

Appendix

Irregular Verb Forms

Base Verb	Simple Past Tense Form	Past Perfect Tense Form
be	was/were	been
become	became	become
begin	began	begun
break	broke	broken
bring	brought	brought
build	built	built
buy	bought	bought
catch	caught	caught
choose	chose	chosen
come	came	come
do	did	done
drive	drove	driven
eat	ate	eaten
fall	fell	fallen
feel	felt	felt
find	found	found
forget	forgot	forgotten
get	got	gotten
give	gave	given
go	went	gone
have	had	had
hear	heard	heard
hit	hit	hit
hold	held	held
hurt	hurt	hurt
keep	kept	kept
know	knew	known
leave	left	left
lend	lent	lent
let	let	let
lose	lost	lost
make	made	made
meet	met	met
pay	paid	paid
put	put	put
read	read	read
ride	rode	ridden
ring	rang	rung
rise	rose	risen
run	ran	run

Base Verb	Simple Past Tense Form	Past Perfect Tense Form
say	said	said
see	saw	seen
sell	sold	sold
send	sent	sent
show	shown	shown
sit	sat	sat
speak	spoke	spoken
spend	spent	spent
stand	stood	stood
swim	swam	swum
take	took	taken
teach	taught	taught
tell	told	told
think	thought	thought
throw	threw	thrown
understand	understood	understood
wear	wore	worn
write	wrote	written

Gerunds and Infinitives

Verbs Usually Followed by Gerunds	Verbs Usually Followed by Infinitives	Expressions Followed by Gerunds
discuss	agree	certain of
dislike	choose	good at
enjoy	decide	interested in
feel like	hope	sorry about
finish	learn	tired of
keep	need	unsure about
miss	plan	used to
practice	promise	worried about
quit	want	
suggest		
understand		

Vocabulary List

(The numbers refer to units where words first appear.)

abuse (10)

academic (4)

actually (7)

adjust (4)

admission (3)

adopt (7)

affect (9)

affordable (8)

agent (8)

agreement (6)

alternative (6)

anthropologist (6)

apiece (7)

appliance (10)

application (3)

approve (8)

architect (2)

architecture (2)

arrange (1)

arrest (10)

artery (5)

aspirin (5)

assistance (3)

assistant (4)

attitude (10)

availability (4)

bark (5)

better-paying (3)

beyond (2)

blaze (1)

blood (5)

brand-new (8)

breadwinner (9)

bride (10)

bundle of money (4)

burial (1)

caregiver (9)

carpentry (7)

case (10)

cattle (6)

chemical (5)

childhood (9)

choose (9)

clerical (3)

closing date (8)

comic book (7)

common (5)

community (8)

community college (3)

computer science (3)

condition (8)

conscious (9)

consider (8)

contest (2)

contract (8)

convict (10)

court (10)

courtyard (1)

credit (8)

crime (10)

crowded (4)

cubic feet (2)

cure (5)

currently (3)

data processing (3)

daybreak (1)

defense (10)

design (N) (2)

design (V) (2)

designer (2)

destroy (6)

determination (7)

devastated (8)

develop (5)

disappear (6)

disease (5)

distant (2)

divorce (9)

divorcée (9)

doctorate (7)

dome (1)

domed (1)

donor insemination (9)

dormitory (4)

dowry (10)

dusk (1)

eager (3)

economic (6)

economically (9)

effort (6)

elevator (7)

emotion (9)

emperor (1)

employment (3)

encourage (3)

encyclopedia (7)

enroll (4)

enrollment (4)

enter (4)

entry (2)

especially (3)

estimate (8)

except (7)

expect (2)

expense (8)

experience (2)

explore (9)

farthest (7)

fatherhood (9)

fight (5)

financial aid (3)

flexibility (4)

float (1)

focus (5)

forget (6)

formal (7)

freshman (4)

further (3)

future (3)

gate (1)

GED (7)

glow (1)

gold (6)

graduate (ADJ) (4)

graduate (V) (7)

granite (2)

grave (1)

greed (10)

greedy (10)

groom (10)

healing arts (6)

heart (5)

herb (6)

high school equivalency test (7)

honor (V) (2)

honor (N) (10)

housing project (8)

human rights (10)

ideal (10)

improve (3)

in the bargain (4)

income (8)

increase (4)

industry (4)

inscription (1)

inspection (8)

inspector (8)

intent (8)

interest rate (8)

jewel (1)

law (10)

lawyer (10)

lending agency (8)

leukemia (5)

librarian (7)

literature (7)

local (8)

lose (6)

lower (4)

lower-income (8)

lucky (9)

lung cancer (5)

malaria (5)

marriage (10)

master's (7)

mature (9)

memorial (1)

middle-income (8)

minaret (1)

mine (6)

mineral (6)

minor (8)

mortgage (8)

motherhood (9)

mystery (1)

native people (6)

nature (6)

negotiate (8)

networking (4)

odd (7)

offer (V) (4)

offer (N) (8)

office assistant (3)

oil (6)

on-line (4)

opportunity (3)

opposed to (9)

organization (6)

palace (1)

panel (2)

partner (9)

passion (10)

payment (10)

peaceful (1)

percentage (6)

perfect (8)

personal (2)

pharmacy (5)

pilgrim (1)

pious (1)

placement service (3)

plaque (5)

platform (1)

poorly (7)

popular (4)

position (10)

prescription drug (5)

prevent (5)

primary (9)

prison (10)

private (2)

process (8)

professional (2)

professor (4)

profit (6)

profitable (6)

program (3)

programming (4)

promise (6)

protect (10)

provide (8)

public (2)

punishment (10)

purchase price (8)

put down (8)

qualified (8)

quality (4)

quinine (5)

raise (7)

react (2)

real estate (8)

reasonable (8)

recall (7)

recent (10)

recommend (8)

redefine (9)

rediscover (5)

reflective (2)

relationship (9)

remain (1)

remarkable (7)

remarry (10)

repairs (8)

request (3)

required (8)

research (4)

role (9)

romance (1)

root (5)

rural (7)

safe (8)

scholarship (7)

separate (7)

serious (8)

settle down (3)

share (6)

shocked (7)

silent (1)

single (9)

skills (3)

smaller (4)

society (10)

sociology (7)

soldier (2)

source (5)

species (5)

specifically (10)

spouse (10)

stressful (9)

student loan (3)

suitable (8)

sunrise (1)

sunset (1)

support (9)

survival (5)

take advantage of (3)

technology (4)

tomb (1)

traditionally (9)

train (3)

transfer (4)

treat (5)

treatment (5)

trial (10)

tribe (6)

tropical (5)

tuition (4)

unfortunately (10)

unmarried (9)

unsure (9)

untraditional (9)

unusual (6)

upgrade (3)

urge (7)

value (N) (5)

value (V) (6)

violation (10)

widow (9)

wife (wives) (9)

with his hands (7)

worn-out (7)

yard sale (7)

Skills Index

LANGUAGE (Grammar, Usage, and Mechanics)

WRITING

VOCABULARY

MAP WORK